Talk L

D1632989

WEEK LOAN

Other titles of interest:

Speaking Frames – Year 3/4/5/6
Sue Palmer
1-84312-109-3/1-84312-110-7/1-84312-111-5/1-84312-112-3

Teaching Speaking and Listening in the Primary School
E. Grugeon, L. Hubbard, C. Smith and L. Dawes
1-85346-785-5

Teaching Thinking Skills Across the Early Years
Belle Wallace
1-85346-842-8

Talk Box

Speaking and Listening Activities for Learning at Key Stage 1

Lyn Dawes and Claire Sams

 **David Fulton** Publishers

This book is for

Anna, Joshua, Eleanor
Neil and Paul

with our love

David Fulton Publishers Ltd
The Chiswick Centre, 414 Chiswick High Road, London W4 5TF

www.fultonpublishers.co.uk

First published in Great Britain in 2004 by David Fulton Publishers

10 9 8 7 6 5 4 3 2 1

David Fulton Publishers is a division of Granada Learning Limited, part of ITV plc.

Note: The right of Lyn Dawes and Claire Sams to be identified as the authors of this work has been asserted by them in accordance with the Copyright, Designs and Patents Act 1988.

British Library Cataloguing in Publication Data
A catalogue record for this book is available from the British Library.

ISBN 1-84312-202-2

Designed and typeset by Kenneth Burnley, Wirral, Cheshire
Printed and bound in Great Britain

Contents

Acknowledgements

The Thinking Together team at the Open University contributed to the ideas behind this book and helped to create its content. We have much appreciated their support in its production. Thank you to Dr Karen Littleton, Professor Neil Mercer, Denise Rowe and Dr Rupert Wegerif.

We would also like to thank Pam Burns for her constant and utterly reliable administrative support.

In addition we would like to thank all the teachers who have helped us by offering suggestions for lessons and by using the developing lessons with their classes. In particular we would like to mention the dedicated Milton Keynes teachers who took part in the Open University's Esmee Fairburn Talk Box project:

> Knowles First School – Head Margaret Morris, Jan McCluskey, Ranjit Basra

> Moorland First School – Head Margaret Fo, Sam Ellison

> Wyvern First School – Head Steve Hopkinson, Margaret Persaud, Diane Norton, Karen Westley

We would also like to thank all the staff at Woolmore School, East London. Supported by Head Teacher Tracy Argent, Woolmore teachers implemented the Thinking Together Talk Box approach throughout the school, and invited us to see (and hear) what a brilliant effect it can have when undertaken with enthusiasm and imagination. We enjoyed an afternoon that left us full of admiration for both teachers and children.

The structure for Lesson 14 was kindly contributed by Denise Rowe, Project Leader for the Esmee Fairburn Talk Box project.

Finally we want to thank our families for everything they did to make Talk Box possible. In particular, Anna did the artwork for the original lessons, Joshua helped with suggestions for Talk Box Rules and Eleanor listened to the stories.

Lyn Dawes and Claire Sams

Notes about the contributors

Lyn Dawes is a primary teacher specialising in spoken language, science and ICT. From 1997 to 2000 Lyn undertook research investigating the integration of computers into classrooms, subsequently working for the British Educational Communications and Technology Agency (Becta) as Education Officer for Software. In 2001 Lyn joined De Montfort University, Bedford, as a Senior Lecturer in Education, working with PGCE and BEd students. Lyn has been involved since 1990 with the Open University's Thinking Together action research programme as teacher-researcher, author and consultant. She contributes regularly to *Junior Education*. Lyn is now a teacher at Middleton Combined School, Milton Keynes.

Claire Sams was a primary school teacher specialising in teaching children with moderate learning difficulties in a mainstream setting. While she was teaching, Claire became involved with the Open University's Thinking Together action research projects. In 2000 Claire joined the Thinking Together research team at the Open University, and managed a KS2 project in Milton Keynes schools on ICT and talk, which focused on Science and Maths. Claire is currently working on the latest Thinking Together project in conjunction with SMILE mathematics. She is a co-author of some teachers' materials and articles relating to the projects. Claire is also an Associate Lecturer working with Teacher Assistants and trainee teachers.

Preface

If teachers are asked what they would hope children gained from their school education, they often include the following: the ability to communicate and work well with other people, and the ability to think and learn effectively alone. These may seem very different kinds of abilities, as the first is to do with language and social interaction, and the second with individual mental activity. However, some recent school-based research – on which this book is based – has shown that they are closely linked. To be more precise, this research has shown how a combination of teacher guidance and group activity can make an important contribution to the development of children's language abilities *and* their thinking skills.

If you record children working together in small groups, as I have often done, you will sometimes capture conversations which are a delight to hear: all the children participate, they pick up each other's ideas and consider them critically. They may disagree, but if so they resolve their differences through further discussion. The group seems to achieve more than the sum of the individual contributions, and the opportunities for participants to learn and to practise effective ways of communicating are quite apparent. The children are 'thinking together'. Such recordings provide good evidence of the educational value of peer group activity. But in most classrooms, those kinds of discussions are unfortunately rare. Most of the time, classroom recordings capture discussions in which children find it hard to listen to each other, in which one person dominates the proceedings, in which children argue unproductively, or in which participants seem happy to go along with whatever anyone says without any reflection or debate. Why should this be so? One likely reason is that, as teachers, we assume that most pupils know how to talk and work together and so we rarely give them explicit guidance or training in how to generate 'good discussions'. We rely on children's social experience to provide them with the resources for thinking together. But that experience may not include much reasoned discussion; they may not understand its value, or know how to use language appropriately.

Spoken language is a powerful tool for learning, which exerts a strong, shaping influence on children's reasoning abilities. But unless children participate in reasoned discussion, of the kind my colleagues and I call Exploratory Talk, we cannot expect to see the beneficial effects of language use on their learning in school and on the development of their thinking skills. An important educational aim, therefore, must be to provide children with well-designed activities in which they learn to use language to think together. This is exactly what the programme of Thinking Together lessons in Talk Box has been designed to do.

Neil Mercer
Professor of Language and Communications
The Open University

Introduction

About Talk Box

Talk Box provides an effective way of teaching children about speaking and listening. The Talk Box lessons are based on years of careful research in schools. They are designed to raise children's awareness of the power of productive talk, enabling them to discuss their work together, and to develop their individual language and reasoning skills. In essence, Talk Box helps to teach children to *think together*. In the classroom, the Talk Box is a real box containing different resources for each lesson. The contents of the Talk Box are used to introduce learning objectives and activities in a way that ensures there is something new, interesting and thought-provoking to start the talk-focused sessions. On completing the series of lessons, children will understand the importance of talk for thinking with others and be more adept at thinking on their own.

Children using Talk Box learn to engage in the educationally effective kind of discussion we call 'Exploratory Talk'. In Exploratory Talk everyone's viewpoint is considered, opinions are justified with reasons and decisions are made together. Speakers and listeners engage critically but constructively with each other's ideas. This sort of talk is very valuable in class because of the way it helps children to reason with one another, clarifying their own thinking and supporting that of their group mates. However, this sort of talk is very rare in most classrooms – it only begins to emerge under the right conditions. These conditions require you, the teacher, and your class to create your own set of 'ground rules' for talking and thinking together. We have listed the kinds of rules that are important below.

Ground rules for exploratory talk

Each person should be invited to speak.
Everyone should listen carefully.
Reasons are asked for, and given.
Agreement and disagreement are accepted as part of the discussion.
Members of a group respect each other's opinions and ideas.
All information is shared.
The group seeks to reach agreement before taking a decision.

Based on these principles, the rules become the class Talk Box Rules. They help children to focus their attention on the way they speak and listen, enabling them to 'think together' and so achieve more by working in a group than each child could alone. A real benefit of this talk is that, as children learn how to reason aloud with others, they learn a pattern of thinking which helps them to reason better when working alone.

You may be reluctant to impose a set of rules for talk on children. But every child in your class will already have their own, implicit ideas about how they should talk and work with others. Unless rules are openly shared and agreed, each child is restricted to their own conception of the nature and purpose of group talk. Widely different assumptions about what it means to talk and work together can generate misunderstanding, disengagement and discord, with the result that group work becomes unproductive and even frustrating for many children. The establishment of shared Talk Box Rules gives everyone the chance to make a useful contribution to joint activity and so enables everyone to think and learn together.

Talk Box lessons

There are 14 lessons divided into two sections:

Section A Lessons 1–5: Establishing the ground rules for talk

Section B Lessons 6–14: Cross-curricular contexts for practising thinking together

It is important to teach Lessons 1 to 5 in the order they are presented. Lessons 6 to 14 can be used in any order.

The lesson activities are designed to be straightforward so that the children can concentrate on the more challenging task of learning to engage one another in Exploratory Talk.

Talk Box contents, resources and learning objectives

Lesson	Title	What's in the Talk Box?	Learning objectives
1	Opening the Talk Box	Talk objects Pictures of talk situations	To raise children's awareness of purposes for talk
2	Talk and listen	Word cards	To consider the importance of active, respectful listening
3	Talk Box badges	Badges Badge templates	To introduce ways of deciding things together in a group
4	You, me, all of us	Classroom equipment Hoops	To talk together to provide information and to consider alternative points of view
5	Our Talk Box Rules	Sports equipment Toy car Pictures, models, toys Traffic lights sheet	To suggest and agree to use a set of rules for talking together
6	Science: similarities and differences	Creature cards Soft toys or model animals	To ask challenging questions, listen and respond
7	Citizenship: choosing presents	Selection of toys	To think about thinking, comparing points of view
8	Pet shop	Models or pictures of pets	To give reasons, evaluate evidence and compare ideas
9	How to Catch a Pig	ICT resource Story resources	To use the ground rules to support problem-solving
10	Literacy: 'Climbing Frame Tag'	Play Park models Story cards Story tape	To discuss issues, asking questions and sharing ideas, and reach agreement
11	Maths: talking about patterns	Patterned paper plane shapes	To use maths vocabulary in discussion
12	Music: sound patterns	Percussion instruments	To talk together to create and share ideas
13	Speaking, listening, learning	Rabbits	*For you to decide*
14	Geography: children around the world	Photographs	*For you to decide*

The Talk Box provides a visual focus and is useful for reminding children that high quality talk is the main aim of the lessons. We hope that you will be able to provide a suitable box. We suggest a cardboard box from the supermarket, or a coloured plastic crate as available in DIY stores, labelled 'Talk Box' and decorated with speech bubbles, talk vocabulary, pictures of people talking and pictures from this book.

Lesson plans include suggestions for specific resources which can be put into the Talk Box in preparation for each session. These include paper-based materials such as worksheets, story cards and pictures, and other resources which we trust are not too difficult to locate. We have tried to keep the resources simple – most of the objects are readily found in school or can be brought in by children – but of course you can provide your own contents to relate to the particular experiences and interests of your class.

Learning objectives and success criteria

The primary learning objective of each lesson is to do with talk. Other learning objectives are to do with curriculum content. The objectives are provided in a teacher version and a 'childspeak' version.

(NB 'Learning objectives' is here used as synonymous with 'Learning intentions' – please use your own preferred terminology with your class.)

Sharing the learning objectives with the children is crucial to the Talk Box approach. This helps children to become aware of the importance placed on their talk together. It is best that this happens near the beginning of the lesson, but not necessarily in the first few moments when it is important to capture the children's interest in the content of the lesson. We have indicated a suitable point in the lesson for sharing learning objectives, but this can be altered to suit the pattern of work in your class.

We have also included success criteria for each lesson. Again these are in 'childspeak', because it is essential that these too are shared with the children. Explicit mention of how to succeed allows everyone to understand what is expected and to work towards achieving the outcomes. The success criteria make it clear to the children what they need to do to meet the learning objectives for the lesson.

A key feature of Talk Box lessons is that learning objectives and success criteria are explained to children and discussed with them.

At any stage in the lesson, the children should be able to say what they are doing, why they are doing it and what they are hoping to achieve.

Lesson structure

The lessons are based on a three-part structure:

- Whole class work 1
- Group work
- Whole class work 2

Whole class work 1

The whole class work at the start of each lesson provides the opportunity:

- for the children to share their ideas and their recall of previous lessons;
- after Lesson 5, to revise the Talk Box Rules;
- for you to introduce the learning objectives;
- for you to provide whole class teaching;
- for you to model the kinds of talk that the children need to use when working in their groups;
- for you and the children to share the success criteria.

Group work

The pair or group activities provide children with the opportunity to:

- use specific ground rules for talk when discussing a meaningful activity;
- practise a particular talk skill, e.g. giving a good reason for a preference, challenging another person's ideas;
- talk to share knowledge and information, and to construct new knowledge together;
- develop confidence and self-esteem through the expectation that they will be equal members of the group with an equal responsibility to contribute to the discussion.

The group activities also give you an opportunity to listen to the children's talk, monitoring the development of their talk skills and their understanding of curriculum content. You may also take up appropriate opportunities to intervene (for example, to model Exploratory Talk, or to check that everyone is being included).

Whole class work 2

The whole class work at the end of each lesson provides the opportunity:

- for the groups to report back to the class;
- for you to pursue lines of reasoning with groups, and expand the discussion to allow a range of contributions from the class;
- for you to address issues that have arisen during the lesson and to make related teaching points;
- to allow you and the children to evaluate the lesson through a review of the success criteria in relation to the learning objectives;
- to allow you and the children to evaluate the usefulness of the Talk Box Rules;
- for you to collect formative assessment information.

Extension work is provided. The learning objectives remain the same or similar, and the class has more practice in each skill. From Lesson 6 on we provide contexts for individual reasoning. This can help you to assess individual progress, and help children to become aware of their own learning in the areas of thinking and reasoning.

Lesson template

For the Talk Box approach to work well, it is best continued beyond the set of lessons we have provided in this book. You can create your own Talk Box-style lessons to fit in with topics and curriculum areas which the members of the class are studying. The Talk Box template (page 5) can be used in this way after Lesson 5. In practice this means generating meaningful contexts for talk in which group work can help children to engage with each other's ideas about the curriculum area. To plan and organise such a 'talking point' per lesson is invaluable.

Using Talk Box in the classroom

Lessons 1 to 5 begin by raising children's awareness of talk as a tool for thinking together. Basic strategies for effective discussion are introduced through the context of activities and stories. These relate primarily to the Speaking and Listening component of the English curriculum, but can be taught whenever seems appropriate.

During Lesson 5 the teacher helps the children to agree on a set of Talk Box Rules. From this stage onwards, children should be able to use the Talk Box Rules in any of their group work. Lessons 6 to 14 are designed to enable the children to apply the Talk Box Rules during activities related to science, maths and other curriculum areas.

The Model for Talk Box (page 5) clarifies the approach.

Key features of the Talk Box thinking together approach

- The learning objectives and success criteria of every lesson must include one or more to do with talking and thinking.
- The objectives should be made explicit to the children before they begin their group work, and their success in achieving them should be discussed afterwards.
- The class should create a set of Talk Box Rules and agree to use them in all group activity.
- The teacher must encourage children's use of Exploratory Talk, help them to understand its nature and purpose, and model it during whole class sessions.

Outcomes of using Talk Box

- Children work more independently, cohesively and collaboratively in groups.
- Children become more aware of how they can use spoken language to think together and get things done.
- More Exploratory Talk is used in class.
- Children become better at reasoning and rational decision-making.
- Children can raise their group and personal achievement in maths, science, literacy and other curriculum subjects.

Talk Box lessons and the curriculum: a model

(you can add other bridging lessons, e.g. into D&T or art; and teach further lessons within the context of a curriculum area)

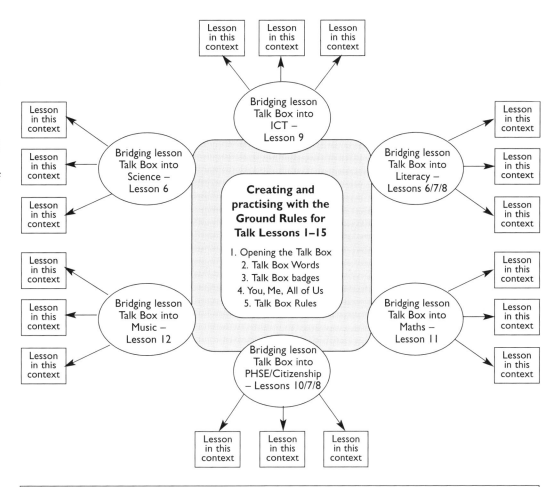

Talk Box template

Lesson title

Resources
In the Talk Box
Other resources (e.g. story cards)

Learning objectives
Objectives for talk
Other objectives (e.g. curriculum-related)
Two versions: one for the teacher, the other written in 'childspeak'
Show and explain the learning objectives for this lesson.

Success criteria
Written in 'childspeak'
Share the success criteria with the children.

Whole class work 1
Introduction by the teacher, using resources from the Talk Box.
Include a reminder of the ground rules and the agreement to use them.

Group work
Discussion in groups using resources provided.

Whole class work 2
Draw out points from group discussion work and relate the outcomes of group work to the introduction and objectives.

Look again at the success criteria.
Use these to discuss whether the learning objectives have been met.
Did the Talk Box Rules help? Should they be altered?

Extension work

Some practical issues

Grouping your class

We recommend mixed-ability and mixed-sex groups of three. This is because we have found that children in friendship groups tend to agree with one another a little too readily. Also, each group needs one person who can read well. However, you know your own class best.

We have found that some Year 1 children do best working in pairs initially, because having to respond to two other people can be too difficult. What is needed is groups in which there is creative friction without too much ease or too much discord. It is helpful to tell individual children that they have been allocated to groups for very positive reasons: because they are good at listening, reading or writing, have good general knowledge or are good at asking questions, good at being encouraging, sensible or including others. The groups should be aware that who reads, writes, uses the mouse and so on is not the focus of attention and brings no particular status. They should also know that it is inappropriate to compete within their group, and that the aim of their group is to talk and work together collaboratively.

Group names (if required) should be decided beforehand and should not occupy the group in discussion during the lesson, unless this is a learning objective. The group is best arranged around the corner of a table, rather than two on one side and one (isolated) opposite.

Collecting resources

'Lesson 1: Opening the Talk Box' asks that you have your Talk Box ready, with picture cards photocopied or collected from your own store and other objects to show the children. Resources for each lesson can either be collected at the start of the series of lessons or as you go along.

Using the Talk Box Rules as often as possible

Once established, the Talk Box Rules can be used to support discussion across the curriculum. If Exploratory Talk is used consistently, this way of working can become an established part of the class ethos. The use of a clear structure for inclusive discussion has been found to benefit group work at the computer in particular.

Talk cards

We have provided a resource sheet to enable you to make talk cards (see page 12). We have found that if children use these as prompts when they are talking in groups, they are much more likely to sustain Exploratory Talk, particularly while they are still becoming familiar with the idea. The use of cue cards is introduced in a structured way in Lessons 1 to 5, but after that you may find that they are useful in other Talk Box lessons, as well as to support discussion across the curriculum

Assessment

The Talk Box lessons provide useful opportunities for formative assessment. Formative assessment can take place while children are in discussion with yourself or each other, as you listen to individuals and collect information about competence, understanding and skills. This can help you to adapt what you have planned to meet the needs you have identified. Children's talk with you during the whole class sessions, or heard during group activities, can be used to assess not only their speaking and listening but also their learning in other curriculum subjects. For example, by listening to a group talking together about science in Lesson 6 you can assess their awareness of how animals can be categorised. Your intervention to challenge misconceptions and provide further information can then be accurately focused.

'Questions for teacher assessment' (page 7) suggests aspects of children's talking and thinking you may wish to focus on. The aims for assessment will affect how these questions are used. You may wish to concentrate on a child or children who have difficulty in speaking and listening, or you may wish to conduct a whole class audit of talk. The list can be used to compile a tally as group work proceeds or as a mental checklist.

Questions for teacher assessment

> **During group work:**
>
> 1. Does the child initiate and carry on conversations?
> 2. Does the child listen carefully?
> 3. Can the child's talk be easily understood?
> 4. Can the child describe experiences?
> 5. Can the child give instructions?
> 6. Does the child follow verbal instructions?
> 7. Does the child modify talk for different audiences?
> 8. Does the child ask questions?
> 9. Does the child give reasons?
> 10. Does the child ask others for their views?
> 11. Does the child reply to challenging questions with reasons?
> 12. Can the child take joint responsibility for decisions?
> 13. Can the child 'think aloud'?
> 14. Can the child generate and consider an alternative point of view?

Each of these questions could be used to consider the child's talk in more detail, by asking more detailed questions. This can be useful if the assessment is to be used diagnostically to identify particular areas of strength or weakness. 'More detailed questions for teacher assessment' takes as an example 'Does the child listen carefully?' and sets out to collect more specific information.

More detailed questions for teacher assessment

> Does the child listen carefully:
>
> * to a familiar adult?
> * to an unfamiliar adult?
> * to friends?
> * to unfamiliar children?
> * when working in a group?
> * in a whole class situation?
> * in a whole school situation?

Self-evaluation by children

Each Talk Box session has evaluation opportunities as part of its plenary. 'Plenary questions' (page 8) includes some questions that can help children to reflect on the quality of their talk.

7

Plenary questions after a Talk Box session

> How did the Talk Box Rules help you to talk about this activity?
> How did sharing your ideas help you?
> How did sharing your ideas help your group?
> Did your group reach a decision? Did the rules help you to do this?
> What were other possibilities? Why did your group reject these?
> Can you provide an example of a good reason/question/challenge you heard today?
> Who did you notice acting as a good listener? How can we tell?
> Did you or any of your group change your mind about something? Can you say why?

Self-assessment using a Talk Diary

More formal self-assessment can be used to build up a comprehensive picture of the child's opportunities to talk with others in a range of contexts. A Talk Diary can focus children on the importance of their talk, providing a useful resource for analysis or reporting. The Talk Diary can be completed, for example, at the end of each Talk Box session, at the end of the day, for a week of term, or intermittently to suit your purposes. A suggested format for the Talk Diary is provided below.

Talk Diary

Name _____ Start date _____

	Talk Box lesson numbers				
	1	2	3	4	5
I talked to the whole class					
I talked in a group					
I asked a question					
I answered a question					
I gave a reason					
I said what I thought					
I listened carefully					
My group talked well					
I joined in					
I liked talking to my group					
I found it hard to talk					
I found it hard to listen					
We could not agree					
We decided together					

References and links

Speaking, listening and learning

The National Curriculum identifies teaching objectives for speaking and listening in 'Use of Language across the Curriculum':

Speaking

In speaking, pupils should be taught to use language precisely and cogently.

Listening

Pupils should be taught to listen to others, and to respond and build on their ideas and views constructively.

Talk Box supports language and literacy development by providing a clear structure for developing children's oral language skills, which feeds into their competence as writers. An extract from the National Literacy Strategy for England and Wales emphasises how important such skills are:

What is Literacy?

Literacy unites the important skills of reading and writing. It also involves speaking and listening which, although they are not separately identified in the Framework, are an essential part of it. Good oral work enhances pupils' understanding of language in both oral and written forms and of the way language can be used to communicate. It is also an important part of the process through which pupils read and compose texts. Thus the Framework covers the statutory requirements for reading and writing in the National Curriculum for English and contributes substantially to the development of speaking and listening.

In collaboration with the National Literacy Strategy, the Qualifications and Curriculum Authority (QCA) in 2003 published *Speaking, Listening, Learning*. This is guidance for teachers wishing to establish a systematic approach to the teaching of speaking and listening.

Speaking, Listening, Learning provides a framework for the direct teaching of explicit skills in the areas of *speaking, listening, group talk* and *drama* with the aim of promoting speaking and listening for learning across the curriculum. The approach identifies skills and sets these out as learning objectives for children in Years 1 to 6, building in opportunities for progression and assessment. The material is informed by the belief that excellent teaching of speaking and listening enhances children's general learning.

Speaking and listening, although inextricably linked, are given separate emphasis. For example, skills for *speaking* include:

Year 1: to describe incidents or tell stories from their own experience in an audible voice
Year 2: to speak with clarity and use intonation
Year 3: to sustain conversation, explaining or giving reasons for their views or choices

Skills for *listening* include:

Year 1: to listen with sustained concentration
Year 2: to listen to others in class, ask relevant questions and follow instructions
Year 3: to follow up each other's points

The *group discussion* guidance includes:

Year 1: to explain their views to others in a small group
Year 2: to ensure everyone contributes
Year 3: to actively include and respond to all members of the group

Skills for *drama* include:

Year 1: to act out their own and well-known stories
Year 2: to adopt appropriate roles in groups
Year 3: to identify and discuss qualities of each other's performance

The guidance provides a clear structure. We believe that the learning objectives should be shared with classes, and that the skills children need to achieve the objectives should be carefully explained and taught. Providing contexts for speaking, listening, group work and drama is essential, but in itself not enough. Talk lessons can ensure that challenging ideas are raised and thoroughly discussed. By employing a Talk Box approach we think that groups of children talking together about a common problem, puzzle, area of interest or concept can be specifically taught to ensure that all members of the group are invited to contribute, and that all contributions are accorded equal respect and consideration. Children learning how to conduct equitable discussion in groups are learning tolerance, through learning how to negotiate their ideas when confronted with alternatives and how to give and evaluate reasons in order to come to a joint understanding.

The guidance offers examples of ways in which speaking and listening objectives can be linked to different subject areas across the curriculum and directs teachers to consider the effect of the way they talk to children. Talk Box supports the QCA guidance by offering a structure for teaching the skills required for group discussion. Through direct teaching of the speaking and listening skills, Talk Box can enhance the quality of children's interaction with one another and with you as a teacher.

Key skills

Of the six key skills that are embedded in the subjects of the National Curriculum for England, Wales and Northern Ireland, Talk Box contributes to learning, practising and developing:

- Communication
- Working with others
- Improving own learning and performance
- Problem-solving

Thinking skills

Talk Box focuses on 'knowing how' as well as 'knowing what' – learning how to learn – and contributes to the development of thinking skills:

- Information-processing skills
- Reasoning skills
- Enquiry skills
- Creative thinking skills
- Evaluation skills

Citizenship links

Talk Box supports the development of good friendships and working relationships between children, as identified in the National Curriculum Statement of Values:

Relationships

We value others for themselves, not only for what they have or what they can do for us. We value relationships as fundamental to the development and fulfilment of ourselves and others, and to the good of the community. On the basis of these values, we should:

- respect others;
- care for others and exercise goodwill in our dealings with them;
- show others they are valued;
- earn loyalty, trust and confidence;
- work co-operatively with others;
- resolve disputes peacefully.

Glossary

Exploratory Talk is talk in which a range of views is carefully considered, reasons are made explicit and decisions achieved jointly. In Exploratory Talk speakers and listeners engage critically but constructively with each other's ideas. Exploratory Talk has special educational value, because its use has been shown to help the development of reasoning.

Ground rules for talk are a set of rules agreed by a teacher and class and used during any group activity.

Talk Box Rules are the ground rules for talk generated by a teacher and class as they work through the Talk Box lessons. The Talk Box Rules are intended to increase the use of Exploratory Talk and so help children 'think together' more effectively.

References and further reading

Clarke, S. (2001) *Unlocking Formative Assessment*. London: Hodder and Stoughton.

Dawes, L., Wegerif, R. and Mercer, N. (2000) 'Extending Talking and Reasoning Skills using ICT', in M. Leask (ed.) *Learning to Teach with ICT in the Primary School*. London: Routledge.

Dawes, L., Wegerif, R. and Mercer, N. (2000) *Thinking Together: Activities for Key Stage 2 Children and Teachers*. Birmingham: Questions Publishing.

Dawes, L. (2001) 'Interthinking: the power of productive talk', in P. Goodwin (ed.) *The Articulate Classroom*. London: David Fulton Publishers.

Grugeon, E., Hubbard, L., Smith, C. and Dawes, L. (1998) *Teaching Speaking and Listening in the Primary School*. London: David Fulton Publishers.

Mercer, N. (1995) *The Guided Construction of Knowledge*. Clevedon: Multilingual Matters.

Mercer, N. (2000) *Words and Minds*. London: Routledge.

Qualifications and Curriculum Authority (2003) *Speaking, Listening, Learning: Working With Children in Key Stages 1 and 2*. London: HMSO (Ref DfES 0625/0626/0627-2003).

Wegerif, R. and Dawes, L. (2001) 'Talking Solutions: The role of oracy in maximising the educational potential of ICT', in M. Monteith (ed.) *Teaching Primary Literacy with ICT*. Exeter: Intellect Books.

Wegerif, R. and Dawes, L. (2004) *Thinking and Learning with ICT*. London: Routledge.

Web links

Thinking Together www.thinkingtogether.org.uk

The National Curriculum www.nc.uk.net

Relationships and the National Curriculum http://www.nc.uk.net/language.html

Becta Information Sheets www.becta.org.uk

DfES Standards Site for Speaking, Listening, Learning www.dfes.gov.uk (search under Primary National Strategy)

References relate to the English National Curriculum, but the ideas in this approach are appropriate for all children of this age range.

Talk cards   Each group will need one or more copies of these cards for the lessons stated. They can be pasted back to back if required, or be on separate cards.

Lesson 2

talk	listen

Lesson 3

What do you think?	Why do you think that?

Lessons 4 and 5

I agree, because . . .	I don't agree, because . . .

Lesson 1 Opening the Talk Box

In the Talk Box	• Talk picture cards (Worksheet 1) • Real or toy telephone; mobile phone; microphone; megaphone; story tape; board game; children's comic or joke book; playing cards; computer game • Example of classroom worksheet which requires collaboration

Learning objective

To raise children's awareness of talk and its purposes.

We are learning to talk about talk.

Success criteria

I can share ideas about ways we use talk.

Whole class work 1

Show and explain the learning objectives for this lesson.

Begin with a whole class discussion about how we learn to talk and the things people do with talk. Some starting points are:

- Who thinks they are a talkative person?
- Who thinks they are a quiet person?
- Who do you like talking to? Why?
- When are you asked not to talk? Why?
- What does 'chatterbox' mean?
- When is it really helpful to be able to talk together? Why?
- When is it difficult to talk to other people?
- What do you like to talk about with your friends?
- What sort of things can we do in school by talking together?
- How did you learn how to talk? Are you still learning?
- What sorts of things can we do with talk (e.g. ask a question, ask for help, share what we know, talk about something to understand it better, make each other laugh, give instructions)?

Show the children the Talk Box. Ask for volunteers to come and take out items. Ask them to explain to the rest of the class how the objects are connected with talk.

What do we use talk for? How do we learn to talk?

Next, ask individual children to take out a picture card and say what they can see happening.

Ask the class to say what sort of talk is happening (argument, persuasion, chat, telling information, asking questions and so on).

Group work

Arrange the class into their groups of three.

Share the success criteria with the children.

Give each group one of the picture cards and ask them to talk together to decide:

What is happening? What are the people saying? What will happen next?

Whole class work 2

Either make up the talk as they imagine it or make up a story to explain what the talk is about.

Ask the children to decide who will report back for their group.

Ask each group to report back on what talk they thought might be happening in their picture. Bring out the idea that we use talk for a range of purposes and that without talk, people find things very difficult indeed. Ask children if they can speak more than one language, and stress that this is admirable.

Ask the children to say how well they worked together in their group. Who made a good suggestion?

Who was a good listener? What are the advantages of working in a group? Explain that teachers ask children to work in groups because talk together helps everyone to develop their ideas.

Use the success criteria to discuss whether the learning objectives have been met.

Extension activities

1. Read the story, 'Bracken Asks Some Questions'. Resources in the Talk Box could include puppets or soft toys of the characters, or paper finger puppets of rabbits for each child to wear. Use the story as a stimulus to discuss problems children may have encountered with talk: what happens when people do not ask questions, share what they know or discuss their ideas? Why do people (adults and children) not listen, sometimes?

2. Ask the groups to think about the picture cards again. This time, have enlarged photocopies of the cards. Ask the groups to draw and make up the contents of 'speech bubbles' for each person. Add another person and what they say. Finally decide on a title for the picture. Emphasise that an important part of this activity is to talk to one another to decide on the group's best idea.

3. Ask the children to find out about their talk history. What was their first word? Who taught them to talk? Has anyone got a younger brother or sister who says funny things?

4. Ask the children to think of someone they like to talk to. Draw a picture of this person. Add a sentence to say what things make this person good to talk to. Is there someone who they like to have talking to them? What makes this person a good talker?

5. Ask the children to make the link between speaking and listening. Why is it important to listen to others? What difference does it make if you listen carefully? Can you listen and think at the same time about what people are saying?

Bracken Asks Some Questions

Fluff the rabbit was searching for dandelions to make juice. She was looking worried. Her ears drooped and her whiskers were all wobbly. The very famous travelling rabbit Banjo Bunny had arrived to entertain everyone with a concert. At this very moment he was resting in the guest burrow. The trouble was, he liked to sing very long songs all evening. Like all her friends, Fluff wasn't very keen on Banjo Bunny's songs.

'They are so strange, and they give everyone earache!' she thought, rubbing her ears. 'But he only does it to be kind and to repay us for letting him stay for the night. I wish he wouldn't. Everyone wishes he wouldn't. Oh, dear. It's going to be very difficult.' She shook her paws and carried on frowning and filling her basket with flowers.

Bracken was skipping around the field in the afternoon sun. He liked skipping, but it was very hot in his fur coat.

'I wonder if I can have a drink,' he said to himself, running home. His home was the biggest round hole under the blackthorn hedge. He took a deep breath and shouted down the hole,

'Mum! Mum! Where are you? MUM!'

'What? What's wrong?' His mum, who was called Toffee, appeared out of the ground in panic.

'Mum! Can I have a drink of water?'

'Oh, for goodness sake, Bracken! I was right in the middle of my crossword. Of course you can have a drink. You don't have to ask for it. Just get yourself one without making so much fuss!'

'Oh! Sorry,' said Bracken. Toffee vanished again and Bracken went to the kitchen for some water. Then he went outside again to carry on skipping. Soon a large grey cloud came and covered the sun and a rather chilly wind began to blow over the field. Bracken felt shivery. He ran back to the burrow.

'Mum! Mum! Where are you? MUM!'

'I'm here, I'm here! What's happened?' Toffee rushed out of the burrow looking around anxiously.

'Mum! Can I put my coat on?'

'Oh, Bracken, is that all? Why ever not? You don't have to ask to put your coat on. Just do it! Now you've made me miss the end of my programme.'

Bracken's ears drooped. 'Sorry Mum,' he said. He had actually asked about his coat in the hope that his Mum would go and fetch it, because he had no idea where it was. He would have to do without. He hopped outside again.

At the edge of the field, next to the hedge, he saw Fluff setting out the stage for Banjo Bunny's concert. She had collected a row of logs for the biggest rabbits to sit on and made sure that there was room at the front for the little ones. Mittens the cat, her kitten Liffey, and her friends Tibby and Baggins were already sitting on the lowest branch of the oak tree waiting for the show to begin. Higher up still were seven inquisitive squirrels. Quite a few small hedgehogs were collected around the edge of the stage.

Bracken noticed Mr Whistle the blackbird up in the blackthorn bush, trying out some tunes. He stood still to listen.

'That is so good,' Bracken said admiringly. 'Hey! Mr Whistle! HEY!'

Mr Whistle stopped in the middle of a song.

'What? What? What?' he said, peering through the branches.

'Hey, can I whistle too?' said Bracken. 'Can I?'

'Is that why you stopped me, to ask that?' said Mr Whistle crossly. 'You dopey creature. If you want to whistle, you just do. It's one of those things you don't have to ask about. Anyone can whistle if they feel like it. You just blow. Now what was that tune . . .' He started trying out notes again, and was soon whistling a complicated and very interesting tune. Bracken joined in, though if you had been listening, you would have noticed that rabbits can't whistle as beautifully as blackbirds.

Banjo Bunny woke up and stretched and yawned and sniffed a little. He started to think what songs he would sing at the concert. He decided to sing some nice sea songs. He had forgotten that none of the rabbits had ever seen the sea.

'I could do with a night off singing,' he said to himself. 'But I can't let everyone down. I'd better make an effort.' There was a tap at the door of the guest burrow and Fluff appeared.

'Hello! I've left you some dandelion juice on the table,' she said.

'Thank you,' said Banjo.

By now Bracken really was too chilly. He went back into the burrow. On the table was a large glass with a nice pale-coloured liquid in it.

'Hmmm,' thought Bracken. 'Now what did Mum say? You don't have to ask if you want a drink . . .'

He took a small sip of the golden juice. It was delicious. In two minutes he had finished drinking it all. He rinsed the glass and, because he was a very thoughtful rabbit, he filled it up again with water. Then he noticed an unusual white furry coat hanging on the chair. It had clover-leaf buttons and two big pockets.

'Hmmm,' thought Bracken. 'What did Mum tell me about coats? If you want to put one on, just do it!' He pulled on the warm white coat and suddenly felt better. He hopped outside.

'Hey, Bracken,' called his friend Liffey the kitten. 'Cool coat! Come and play with me till the concert starts? I'm going to do a bit of digging in the sand pit!'

As the sun went behind the oak tree, Fluff found spaces for all the rabbits to see the concert. Down in the guest burrow, Banjo Bunny got up and brushed his whiskers and combed his ears. He made his way to the kitchen and sipped at the drink on the table.

'This is very unusual dandelion juice,' he thought. 'Now where is my coat?'

Toffee came in to see if he was ready. Both of them searched for the lost coat, but they couldn't find it anywhere. Banjo found a blue patchwork coat with a hood behind the door.

'That's Bracken's,' said Toffee. 'Why not borrow it and we can find yours later?' Banjo was quite pleased with the patchwork coat. Up he went, and stood before the rabbits, cats, hedgehogs and squirrels, and bowed. All the creatures clapped with their quiet soft paws. Banjo bowed again and began to sing.

'Oowwwoo, oowwwoooo,' he sang. 'There was a bunny had a tale, she sailed across the sea, woo woo . . . Oh where are you, my bunny boy, with yer whiskers ninety-three oow woo . . .'
    Fluff wished she could put her paws in her ears, but that wouldn't be very polite.
    Toffee tried hard to think of crossword clues that she hadn't solved, to take her mind off the noise. The littlest rabbits crouched down in the grass and shivered.
    Mr Whistle took fright and flew away making a loud angry 'Chit! Chit!' sound.

Across the field, in the sandpit, Liffey and Bracken heard the song.
    'What is that terrible racket?' said Liffey. 'Sounds like someone's being eaten alive.'
    'Shut up, Liffey, it's the concert,' said Bracken, 'We'd better go or there will be trouble. The rule is if you don't go to the concert, you don't get any supper.' He stood up and brushed down the coat, which was now more sandy-coloured than white.
    'You look like a fox!' said Liffey.
    'Shh! Come on. We'll creep up and get places at the back,' said Bracken.

Banjo was just starting his third song as they slipped into their places.
    'Now this is a jolly tune!' said Banjo, and he started singing:
    'Bobby Rabbit's gone to sea-eee with shiny ears and big white tee-eeth . . . !' The audience looked very baffled and trembled with each word.
    'Hmmm!' thought Bracken. 'I recognise that coat. Banjo's right, it is a jolly tune, but no one seems very lively. I wish I could join in. Now what did Mr Whistle tell me? You don't have to ask if you want to whistle . . . anyone can whistle if they want to – you just blow!' He put his nose up, took a deep breath, closed his eyes very tight and started whistling along with Mr Banjo's song as loudly as he could.

Hearing the most horrible shriek, all the rabbits' ears shot up in astonishment.
The little ones at the front turned round, caught a glimpse of fox-coloured coat and scattered into the night.
The hedgehogs curled into a row of spiky balls like sea urchins.
Mittens, Tibby and Baggins jumped in surprise. 'Wow! What a wonderful noise!' they thought, joining in immediately with a terrible wailing sound.
Liffey fell off his log laughing and lay helpless on the grass.
In an instant Fluff and Toffee decided that whistling was a brilliant idea. They too put their noses up towards the sky, took a deep breath, closed their eyes tight, and began a very loud and very unmusical singing.

Banjo, who had been a bit dismayed by the rows of silent rabbits, suddenly felt a lot better as his audience joined in. Picking up his tambourine he began bashing it gaily. In a moment all the rabbits were hopping, whistling and singing along. It was a great concert. It lasted for three hours and Banjo took four encores at the end. Bracken whistled and whistled. He got so warm that he took off the fox-coloured coat, and the seven squirrels slipped down and stole it away to make waistcoats for winter. Liffey got bad hiccups and was taken off to have his tail dipped in the stream to calm him down. The little rabbits gradually crept back, the hedgehogs uncurled and began to dance, and even Mr Whistle added his voice to the songs.

'Everyone come and have some dandelion juice,' said Fluff, and Banjo never did work out why the glass after the concert was so strong and sweet. His missing coat was also a mystery.

The next morning Bracken sat by the gate to wave Banjo off on his journey. Liffey was sitting neatly on the gate post. They were very surprised when not only Banjo appeared, but Fluff as well.

'I'm going along too, to collect some songs about fields and hedgerows for next year's concert,' Fluff said.

'You can keep my coat, Banjo,' said Bracken. 'I hope it brings you luck.'

They waved till Fluff and Banjo hopped out of sight, then Liffey jumped off the gate post and stretched enormously.

'Hey Bracken, do you want a race?' said Liffey, ready to rush away.

'You don't need to ask!' said Bracken, and with a big leap he set off down the field.

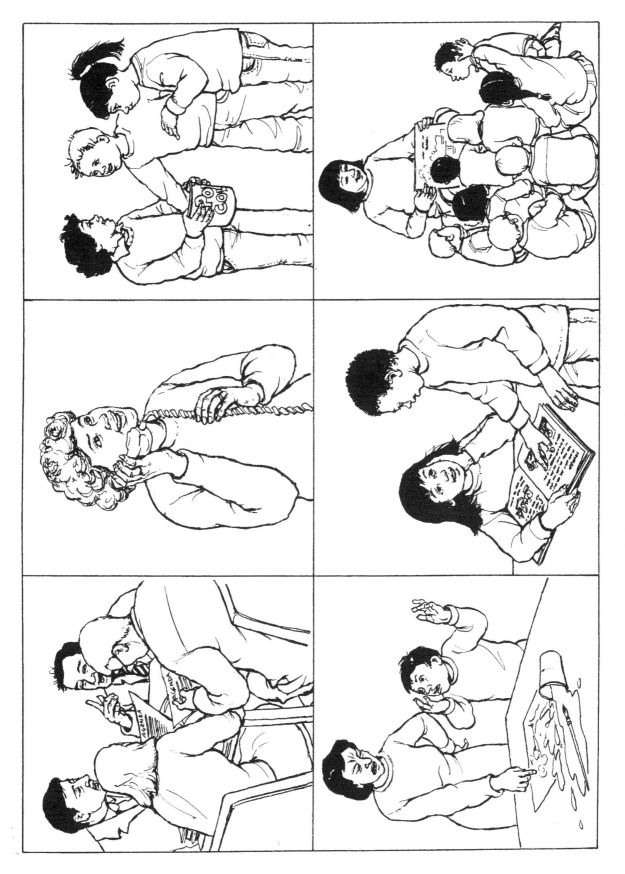

Worksheet I Talk picture cards

Lesson 2   Talk and listen

In the Talk Box	• Pictures or models of animals with big ears (elephant, rabbit, fox) • Word cards (Worksheet 2) photocopied on card and cut up • Talk cards 'Talk' and 'Listen' (page 12) • Timer

Learning objective

To increase children's awareness of the importance of listening to each other.

We are learning to listen carefully to each other.

Success criteria

I can listen to my partners talking then tell other people what the talk was about.

Whole class work 1

Ask for volunteers to choose an animal from the box. Why do they have big ears? What are they listening for? Why do we have sensitive ears? What sort of sounds can we hear? What does 'listen!' really mean? How can you tell when someone is listening? What can go wrong when people do not listen carefully? Can the class give an example of being asked to listen or asking someone to listen to them?

Ask children to take word cards out of the box and with the help of the class say what they think their word means. Can they use the words in a sentence? Explain that these words are all connected with talk and that speaking and listening are both important things to learn, especially if you are going to do well in the classroom.

Show and explain the learning objectives for this lesson.

Group work

Arrange the children in groups of three and designate children as 'red, yellow, green' or 'a, b, c' so that turn taking is organised. Explain that you are going to time them for one minute; use a sand timer or an electronic timer so all can either see or hear. In that minute the 'red' person is going to tell the others about something. It could be a pet, a brother or sister, a favourite toy, game or TV programme, a recent shopping or cinema trip, or perhaps a birthday. (You may want to draw a picture or hold up an object to symbolise these topics, e.g. toy animal, cinema ticket, picture of a child, TV set, shopping bag, cake, birthday card.) The other group members must listen carefully. They can ask questions. When one minute has passed, the group will swap roles and repeat the activity.

Use the cue cards (talk, listen) to structure the activity. Each child has a card. One child holds 'Talk' uppermost while the other(s) hold 'Listen' – then swap.

Explain that after this has happened you will ask some of the class to tell everyone about what a member of their group has told them.

Share the success criteria with the class.

Ensure all groups are confident to carry out the listening activity. Now carry out the timed activity. A minute can seem a long time – reduce if it seems necessary.

Whole class work 2

Ask group members to tell the class what they learnt from another person.

Remind the children that the lesson has been about listening as well as talking. Who did they find was a good listener? Why? Who was a good talker? Why?

Collect some ideas together about what makes a good listener, e.g. someone who looks at you while you are talking, someone who sits still, someone who shows you that they are interested in what you have said, someone who asks a question then listens.

Repeat this activity to consider what makes a good talker, e.g. someone who explains things clearly, someone who answers questions well, someone who looks at you when they are speaking.

You might ask the class what we mean when we say things like: 'You can hear what I'm saying but you're not really listening to me.'

Use the success criteria to discuss whether the learning objectives have been met.

Extension activity: Retell a story

Remind the children that they are learning to listen to one another carefully. Read the children the short story 'Liffey's Shopping Trip'.

In the Talk Box
- Empty margarine tub marked 'Butter'
- A pot of strawberry jam
- A box of sugar cubes
- A box of China tea (or box *labelled* 'China Tea')
- Finger puppets – rabbit, kitten – one for each child or group to help with the children's retelling of the story
- Worksheet 2a: Liffey finger puppets

Group work

Ask each group to retell the story to one another. One child can start and then 'pass the story on' to the next until it is complete. Remind the children that they can ask one another for help and ask questions to check whether everyone agrees with the order of the story.

Finally, ask the whole class whether they were able to retell the story in their groups. Did those who were listening interrupt the person who was talking? How did this make them feel? Can interruptions be helpful? How can you let others know that it is all right for them to offer suggestions when you are talking? How can 'turns' in talk be well organised? How important is it to listen carefully or to ask if you need things clarified?

Liffey's Shopping Trip

Liffey was a grey stripy kitten. She wore a red collar and a red woolly hat with holes for her ears. One afternoon her mother, who was called Mittens, was getting ready for her friends Tibby and Baggins to come to tea.

'I have to get out my best cups and make a cake,' said Mittens, who was in a great rush because she had sat out in the sun all morning grooming her coat.

'Liffey, run along to Uncle Raggy's shop for me quickly. Now what do I need? Yes, I need a little packet of butter, a pot of strawberry jam, a box of sugar cubes and some proper China tea.'

'Aren't you going to write it down for me?' said Liffey anxiously.

'No, no, you silly kitten, I don't have time. Here is a purse with the money. Make sure you don't lose it. You can put it under your hat.'

'I will put it in my backpack actually,' said Liffey, who thought she would look really peculiar with a purse under her hat. So she took her red backpack and set off through the wood to the shop.

As she set off, she practised saying to herself,

'A packet of butter, a pot of jam, a box of sugar cubes and some proper China tea!'

On the way she met her friend Bracken the rabbit.

'Where are you going, Liffey?' asked Bracken. 'I have a new skipping rope. Come and play!'

'I am in a hurry,' said Liffey. 'But I suppose five minutes won't matter.' And she skipped and hopped with Bracken for quite a bit longer than five minutes before she remembered her shopping trip. As she set off, she practised saying to herself,

'A packet of butter, a little lot of jam, a box of China straw and some proper sugar, please!'

In the field by the shop she met her friend Dribble the puppy.

'Where are you going, Liffey?' said Dribble. 'I have a new football. Come and play!'

'I am in a hurry,' said Liffey. 'But I suppose five more minutes won't matter.' So she kicked and passed the ball with Dribble for much longer than five minutes before she thought about the shopping. As she set off, she practised saying to herself,

'A cube of China, a very little butter, a box of potato jam, some sugar mice and some proper strawberry tea.'

In the shop it was dark and cool. Uncle Raggy, who was a big ginger cat, was serving Mr Slowly the snail. He was spending ages choosing just the right shade of varnish for his shell. Liffey took the purse out of her backpack and fidgeted about.

'Let's think,' she said to herself. 'It's a good job I've got such a brilliant memory. I know just what I need – I think . . .'

Finally Mr Slowly paid for his varnish and slid out of the shop door.

'Right, Liffey. What can I get for you?' asked Uncle Raggy.

'Ok,' said Liffey. 'Here we go. I want a China pot of cubes, a box of blocks, some strawberry mice, a packet of buttercup jam and some proper sugar, please!'

Uncle Raggy looked a little surprised. But then he smiled at her.

'I see. Well, give me your backpack and I'll put them in,' he said. 'Oh dear, oh dear. I don't think we have many of those things . . . what did you say? A box of socks . . . some ice cream mice . . .' He looked on the shelves and started putting things in the bag.

Suddenly Liffey felt very panicky. What would her mother say if she went home with ice cream mice? It didn't sound quite right. She began to mew. She put her paws over her eyes and rubbed her ears, but it didn't help. It seemed all such a muddle: what on earth were China cubes? And where did the buttercups come in? What had her mother said?

'Oh, I know! It must be ice cubes!' she said excitedly. 'And I mustn't lose them! I must carry them under my hat!'

'Ah yes, of course,' said Uncle Raggy, carefully packing her purse on top of the things he had put in her backpack. 'Ice cubes under your hat. Maybe it will make your ears stiff and help you be a good listener, just like me.' He wrapped some ice cubes in a plastic bag. 'Here. I think you'd better go straight home!'

Liffey shoved the bag under her hat, grabbed her backpack and dashed out of the shop. She felt horrible. Her ears were frozen. Dribble the puppy called her and kicked the ball towards her, but she ignored it. Cold water was running down her face. She sped past Bracken who was waving the skipping rope enticingly. Trickles of ice slipped nastily under her collar. The backpack was terribly lumpy – it must be the – what was it, potato chips, she thought, or the other thing, the . . . the China pot. She bounced into the kitchen and ripped off her red hat.

'There!' she said.

Tibby, Baggins and Mittens looked at her in astonishment. Her fur was wet, and melting bits of ice were slithering all over the floor.

'What have you been up to? You were so long we almost gave up waiting,' said Mittens.

'What have you got there, Liffey?' said Tibby.

But Liffey couldn't have told her. She didn't believe that anyone could have remembered that terrible shopping list. All she could think of was a muddled mixture of how cold her ears were and china pots of buttered mice. Mittens opened the backpack, took out the purse and carefully lifted out what Uncle Raggy had put in.

'Oh! A nice little packet of butter!' she said, sounding very pleased. 'Here we are – a pot of strawberry jam, a good square box of sugar cubes and some proper China tea!'

The visiting cats nodded and looked satisfied. They began to purr.

'What a good kitten your Liffey is,' they said to Mittens, looking forward to their tea.

Liffey went out into the sun to brush her ears and to try to work out what had happened.

What had Uncle Raggy said? That he was a good listener. She wanted to be one too. She rubbed her ears with her paw. Yes, they were nice and stiff now.

Worksheet 2 Talk and listen words

decide	understand
share	interrupt
repeat	persuade
find out	describe
tell	remember
ask	discuss
reason	argue
hear	conversation
think	concentrate
listen	opinion

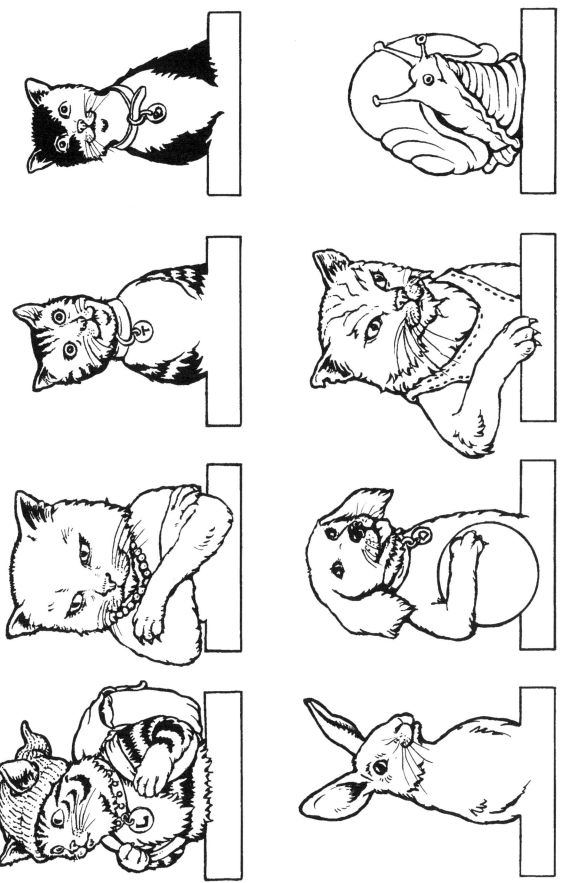

Worksheet 2a   Liffey finger puppets

Lesson 3 | Talk Box badges

Teacher's note

This lesson is effective if it is set in a relevant and topical context for the class. For instance, the badges could be needed for an approaching school trip, assembly or special event, or for children's trays or books. Making a badge could be replaced with designs for bookmarks as part of a school book week. The purpose of the badge design is to allow children to contribute something about themselves to a joint enterprise with their talk group in a non-threatening situation. It is the talk that is the challenge, not the activity. The production of the badge is not actually the main aim of the lesson. This lesson requires children to talk to one another, considering and giving reasons for their preferences, and its objectives are to do with decision-making.

In the Talk Box

- A variety of badges (bookmarks, etc.) for different occasions
- Worksheet 3: Four class badges photocopied onto card and cut up
- Talk cards: 'What do you think?', 'Why do you think that?' (page 12)
- Word cards from Lesson 2
- Extension activity requires paper copies of one badge for each child

---

Learning objective

To learn to make decisions when working in group

Success criteria

> People in my group can listen, give a reason and try to agree.

> We are learning to find ways of deciding together.

Whole class work 1

Ask for volunteers to take badges from the Talk Box and talk about what they show. Now show the class the four badge designs (explain context here if necessary). Explain that the class has to choose one of the four badge designs. Ask the children to put up their hands to show which one they like the best, without conferring, so that there is a range of opinions. Point this out to the children.

Show and explain the learning objective for this lesson.

Discuss with the children what they think might be a *fair* way to decide which badge to choose. Offer some 'possible suggestions'. These might include:

- The oldest child in the class should decide.
- The children wearing blue (etc.) should decide.
- Whichever badge the most people like should be chosen.
- The teacher should decide.
- The children from another class should decide.

Ask the children for their ideas. Then discuss what would be 'fair' and why.

Explain that the class is going to work in groups to talk together to decide which badge should be chosen. Remind the children that they must consider one another's ideas carefully. Also rehearse the talk and listening words introduced in Lesson 2. Show the word cards again to help with this.

Group work

Arrange the class into groups of three and provide the groups with the talk cards. The task now is for one child in the group to ask another which badge they would prefer, by reading out or handing them the cards:

'What do you think?'

'Why do you think that?'

This is repeated until everyone has asked and answered the questions.

The groups continue talking until everyone has had a chance to say what they think.

Remind the children to listen to each other and say whether they agree or disagree with each other's reasons – again saying why.

When they have done this each group should try to agree on one badge. This may mean that some children have to change their minds. Stress that this is a positive thing to do if you have been persuaded by good reasons or new ideas.

Ask the groups to decide who will report back to the class and to make sure that this person can share the group's reasons with everyone.

Share the success criteria with the children.

Whole class work 2

Ask the groups to report back to the rest of the class about which badge they chose. How did they decide? What was the reason for their preference? Discuss any problems that arose in making the decision. Ask how these might be overcome.

After all the groups have reported back, ask the class to agree on one badge for the whole class. Remind them of the strategies for doing this.

Use the success criteria to discuss whether the learning objectives have been achieved.

Extension activity: Joint decision badges

Provide each child with a copy of the class badge. Each child now has to think about their hobbies and interests. Ask the groups to talk together to decide what each might draw on their group version of the badge. For example, in a particular group one child might choose a football; another, a cat; the third, a computer. Each child writes their own name on their badge and draws their object, then passes it to the other two to collect two more drawings. In this way the class ends up with a 'joint decision' badge, and each group has its customised version which says a little about its members.

The badges can be used to wear or stick on to a group folder in which other worksheets and such like may be collected. The children should be aware that the objective of this lesson was to find out about how group decisions are made; the actual badge is not the most important outcome, although the work they have done on it is valued.

Name:
Group mates:

My school is:
My teacher is:
My year is:
My name is:
My group mates are:

Worksheet 3 Class badges

Lesson 4 You, me, all of us

In the Talk Box	• In three separate bags, inside the box:
	  a) Packet of biscuits, an apple, packet of crisps
	  b) Items of sports equipment that represent, for example, football, swimming, gymnastics
	  c) Boxes of three (or more) computer games
	• Three large hoops
	• Blank or prepared label cards for whole class work 1
	• Worksheet 4: one copy for each group
	• Talk cards 'Talk', 'Listen' (page 12)

Learning objectives

To use talk to identify preferences and find out whether these are shared with others.
To categorise on the basis of reasons.
To build group solidarity.

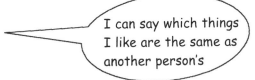

We are learning to talk together to sort things and share ideas.

Success criteria

I can say which things I like are the same as another person's

Whole class work 1

Arrange three hoops on the floor so that they intersect. First label with foods ('Apples', 'Crisps', 'Biscuits'). Now ask a volunteer to take out each of the foods from the Talk Box and show them. Ask the class to decide which they like best, or if they like two or all three equally. Choose children to position themselves in the labelled hoops according to their preferences. Perhaps each child might leave a name card in the hoop they chose.

Now replace the hoop labels with ones relating to sport (football, swimming, gymnastics) and repeat the activity. Finally repeat the activity using computer games (choose three that your class are familiar with). As the children position themselves, ask: What if you like two or more of the items? Where could you put yourself if you do not like any of the things? Have you got any preferences that are the same as someone else?

Show and explain the learning objectives for this lesson.

Group work

Choose one child in each group to be the writer for the group. Explain that the groups are going to use talk to find out about what they like and which of their 'likes' is the same. Display the following questions:

1. 'What do you like doing when you are not at school?'

Using talk cards 'Talk', 'Listen': children take it in turns to ask this question to other group members. They also ask for reasons: 'Why do you like that?' and if possible for further details.

2. 'What is the same about us?'

Ask the children to talk together to find (at least) two things that they have in common with each other. These should be preferences rather than, say, eye colour.

Once the groups have talked for a few minutes they can use the information from these questions to fill in their names and the 'We like' boxes on Worksheet 4. A group sheet should be completed by the designated writer, in discussion with the others.

Share the success criteria with the children.

Whole class work 2

Ask children to talk about their diagrams and share their 'likes' and those of their group with the rest of the class.

Ask the class to evaluate the quality of their group talk. How well did you talk together? Who asked a question? Can anyone remember a reason someone gave? How did you remember to take turns and to listen carefully? How has concentrating on speaking and listening helped everyone with this activity?

Use the success criteria to discuss whether the learning objectives have been achieved.

Extension activity 1: Lend a hand pictures

Learning objective

To reinforce questioning, sharing ideas and reasons, and respecting the opinions of others.

Ask each child to draw round their hands on a piece of A4 paper or do this with one child in advance and photocopy the sheet. Each child should have a clear outline pair of hands.

Ask children to write their name at the top of their sheet.

Each child now thinks of something they like to draw. They do not draw on their own hands sheet, but offer to draw for others (first in their own group, then in the class). For example, they may offer to draw a football, worm, cat, pattern, dog, house, flower or alien on another person's hands sheet. Drawings should be carefully done, and initialled or signed. The owner of the hands must agree that they want the picture being offered. Children can request drawings if they see something they like on a classmate's hands.

When enough contributions have been collected, children return to their groups to finish by drawing their own picture on their own sheet.

Children can be asked to say what they like about the picture they have ended up with. The children should be aware that they are discussing what is being offered, taking decisions and valuing one another's contributions. The Lend a Hand pictures themselves again are not the main outcome, although they can be coloured and displayed if there is free time.

Extension activity 2: Sorting things out

In the Talk Box

- A collection of about ten classroom objects, e.g. scissors, ruler, multilink, book, CD-ROM, pencil, felt-tip pen, dictionary, rubber, sharpener, stapler
- Three large hoops with labels: 'Reading', 'Writing', 'Number'
- Other blank labels

Learning objective

To give reasons for categorisation.

Lay the three labelled hoops on the floor so that they intersect.

Ask the children to take items out of the Talk Box and place them in the position they think is most appropriate. As they place the object, they should give a reason why.

Ask for alternative suggestions about where that object could be placed. For example, does a pencil fit best in one of reading, writing or number? Or is it better where writing and number overlap? Why? Would any object fit in another place if its use were defined differently?

What happens if the names on the labels are changed? For example:

- Materials things are made from: plastic, metal, wood.
- Characteristics of materials: bendy, shiny, hard.
- Other activities: drawing, construction, measuring.

Other contexts

This talk-based activity can be used across the curriculum. Some examples are:

- Science: sorting and classifying materials, or living things
- Literacy: considering attributes of story characters, e.g. kind, unlucky, friendly, bad, good, happy
- Maths: sorting numbers, e.g. in the 2x table; odd and even

I am:

We both like:

I am:

We both like:

We all like:

We both like:

I am:

I am:

Worksheet 4 What we like

Lesson 5 Our Talk Box Rules

Please ensure that you have read the Teacher's notes for this lesson.

Teacher's note

This is the key lesson. The children generate a set of basic ground rules for talk and agree to use them during their group work. These are their 'Talk Box Rules'.
Please refer also to the Introduction, especially 'Talk Box lessons'.

Lessons 1 to 4 have helped to raise the children's awareness of speaking and listening as a means of thinking together, and helped them begin to give and listen to reasons, and to make joint decisions. The following rules encourage educationally effective discussion, or Exploratory Talk.

Ground rules for talk

Each person should be invited to speak.
Everyone should listen carefully.
Reasons are asked for, and given.
Agreement and disagreement are accepted as part of the discussion.
Members of a group respect each other's opinions and ideas.
All information is shared.
The group seeks to reach agreement before taking a decision.

In this lesson, you can help children to decide on their own set of rules, some in their own words, which embody this set of principles. For example, it is extremely important to stress to the children that in talk groups, all opinions will be valued and that all assertions must be backed up with a reason. Also, that constructive challenge and argument must be considered part of Exploratory Talk.

Children often suggest talk rules that are really to do with appropriate behaviour, for example:

'Be quiet in the hall and library.'

'Take care not to shout in the classroom.'

These may be useful rules, but are not directly to do with generating discussion.

Ensure that the children understand this and that they agree to try to talk and think together using their rules, which will be on display in the classroom.

Below is an example of one class's Talk Box Rules.

Our Talk Box Rules

1. Co-operate – try to get along with each other.
2. Take turns to talk and to listen.
3. Share your thoughts.
4. Ask for reasons.
5. Think together about everyone's ideas.
6. Try to reach a shared agreement.

In the Talk Box	• Sports equipment, e.g. bat, ball, swimsuit; baseball cap • A board game • A toy car • Large pieces of paper and marker pens for each group • Worksheet 5: one copy for each group

Learning objective

To establish a set of ground rules for talk.

> We are going to agree a set of rules for talking together.

Success criteria

> We have a set of Talk Box Rules. We all agree to use them.

Whole class work 1

Ask for volunteers to take out items of sports equipment from the box. As each item is removed ask the children to suggest a 'rule' that might be associated with the sport it represents.

- Introduce the concept of 'ground rules' as basic rules that everyone knows.
- Discuss the reasons for rules, emphasising those to do with safety or fairness. What would happen if the rules were changed, e.g. going down ladders and up snakes; sharing out all the Monopoly money? What if only some of the players agreed?
- Bring out the idea that rules do not work unless everyone agrees to use them.
- Use the swimsuit to talk about rules for behaviour at the pool, and the car to ask the children if there are rules for being a passenger as well as being a driver. How are these rules learnt? Some of them are rarely made explicit but are actually well known (e.g. no eating in the pool; not to touch the hand brake).
- Rules can change, e.g. we no longer wear swimming hats although this used to be a rule. Ask the children if they have rules at home for using the television, telephone or computer, or rules to do with talking. For example, a rule might be, 'Don't interrupt when others are talking'.

The aim of this whole class discussion is to ensure that children are aware of the value of rules, that rules are not just restrictions but can help groups of people to be safe (e.g. in cars) or things to be fair (e.g. everyone on a team knows the rules and tries to stick to them to make the game work). It may be important to remind children that the element of competitiveness in games is inappropriate within a talk group of people who are working together to share their thoughts. This is especially true when working with the computer which tends to encourage a 'games' or competitive approach.

Show and explain the learning objective for this lesson.

Now discuss with the class the sort of ground rules they think are important for talk in groups at school. Base the discussion on the example in the 'Teacher's notes'. Children can be encouraged to draw on their experiences of Talk Box Lessons 1 to 4.

When talking together, what worked in their groups? What went wrong? Who is good at speaking and listening? How do we know? What rule would help your group to work together well?

Encourage the children to consider the idea that talk helps thinking. Bring out the ideas that in group talk all opinions will be valued, that questions must be asked and that all opinions must be backed up by a *reason*.

Group work *Share the success criteria with the children.*

Provide one copy of Worksheet 5 for each group. Ask the reader to read out each box in turn, then all the group must talk together, giving opinions and reasons, to decide whether this is:

- a sensible rule for group talk (colour green)
- not a sensible rule (colour red)
- unsure or undecided (colour orange) (it is fine to be undecided as long as that is the group's decision!)

Talk cards can be use to structure the discussion if necessary.

Whole class work 2 Ask each group to report back on the rules that they felt were important. You might want to fill in a tally chart so that the children can see which rules everyone agrees on. Check for overlaps and consensus within the class. Decide on a set of rules. In addition, discuss the children's original rules (written in the circles) and incorporate these into your list if the class agree. Try to use the children's phrasing where possible.

The rules you end up with should strongly reflect the ground rules provided in the 'Teacher's notes'. It may be necessary to streamline the list – too many rules would be confusing.

Ask the children if they think it is a good idea to agree to use these shared ground rules for talk when working in groups. How would it help? Are there any further suggestions or modifications? Introduce the phrase 'Talk Box Rules' as shorthand for describing the set of rules which generates Exploratory Talk.

Use the success criteria to discuss whether the learning objectives have been met.

After the lesson, make a poster of the rules and display it in the classroom. Provide copies for children to take home. Ask parents for their response. Ensure that the rules are posted around the computer room. Ask children to collect examples of when the rules have been useful to share with you and the class. From Lesson 5 onwards, this set of rules can be constantly referred to and used to help children share their thoughts and ideas.

Extension activity 1: Story illustration **Learning objective**

To practise using the Talk Box Rules.

If this has not happened already, read the short story 'Liffey's Shopping Trip' in Lesson 2.

If the class has heard the story, briefly ask them to remind one another what happens.

The task is for groups to draw a picture together to illustrate one scene in the story.

They must use their ground rules to choose a scene and decide how to work together to create a picture. For example, they can all draw on one large piece of paper; they can draw and cut out separate bits of the scene; they can use the computer. Ask the groups to create a picture with a caption and one or more speech bubbles. Ask the children if they can remember what Liffey decided at the end of the story.

Scenes which can be illustrated in this way are:

- Liffey sets off on the shopping trip
- Liffey plays skipping with Bracken the rabbit
- Liffey plays football with Dribble the dog
- In Uncle Raggy's shop
- Liffey arrives home with the shopping

Ask the groups to explain how they used the ground rules to reach their decision about which scene to draw and about how to work together on the task. Which rules do they think they were best at using? Were there any that they found hard? Do they think that they did better as a group than they could have done working alone?

Extension activity 1: Talk about our ideas

Learning objective

To practise using the Talk Box Rules.

Provide each group with a copy of the 'I agree because' and 'I don't agree because' talk cards.

Activity (a)

Choose a current whole school issue. Provide the children with a statement or question. (For example, 'Footballs should be banned from the playground' ; 'People who drop litter should be asked to stay after school to help clear it up'; ' We should only be allowed chips for lunch once a week.')

Activity (b)

Choose one (or more) of the statements below, enlarge, display and explain it.

Children should walk to school.

We should be taught keyboard skills instead of handwriting.

We should not learn maths, just learn to use calculators.

Everyone should have the same amount of pocket momey each week, paid by the government.

Children should be able to choose their own bedtime.

Children should be given sweets or chocolate for lunch.

Children should be taught to swim.

Children should not have to wear school uniform.

School holidays should be longer.

Group work

Each child in turn takes the 'I agree because' card, repeats the phrase and offers a reason why they agree with the statement. Children can discuss which they think are sensible or fair reasons. Each child takes the 'I don't agree because' card and shares a reason.

Groups then use all the ideas they have heard to talk together and decide what their group thinks. Ask each group to report back on their decisions and reasoning. Decide whether the ground rules for talk helped the discussions. Should the rules be modified?

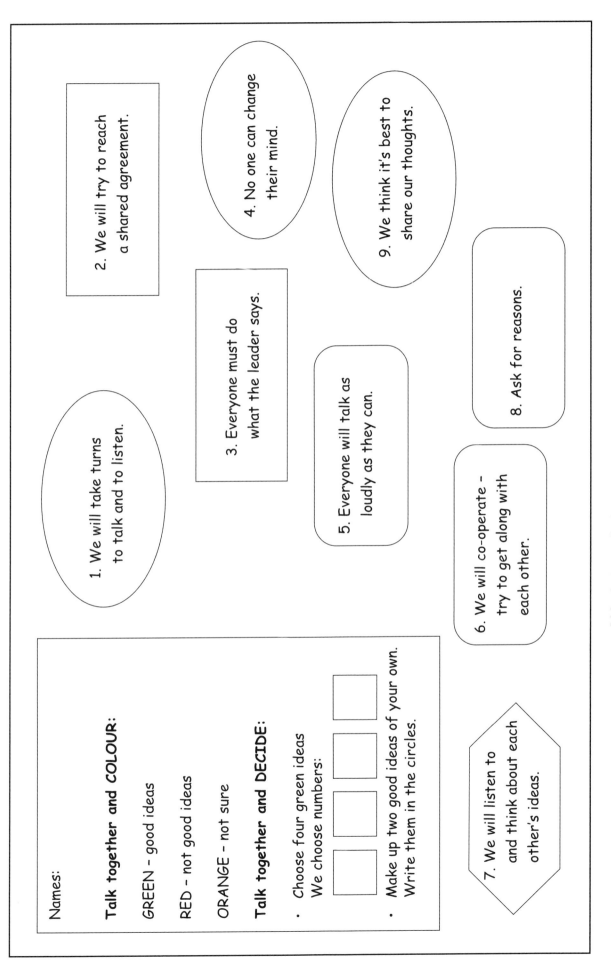

2. We will try to reach a shared agreement.

4. No one can change their mind.

9. We think it's best to share our thoughts.

3. Everyone must do what the leader says.

1. We will take turns to talk and to listen.

5. Everyone will talk as loudly as they can.

8. Ask for reasons.

6. We will co-operate – try to get along with each other.

7. We will listen to and think about each other's ideas.

Names:

Talk together and COLOUR:

GREEN – good ideas

RED – not good ideas

ORANGE – not sure

Talk together and DECIDE:

• Choose four green ideas
We choose numbers:

☐ ☐ ☐ ☐

• Make up two good ideas of your own. Write them in the circles.

Worksheet 5 Talk Box Rules: traffic lights

Our group's ideas

10. The person who is writing chooses what happens.

11. If people find it had to join in, we can ignore them.

12. We will keep our ideas quiet so that no one else can copy.

13. The person who speaks first will decide what to do.

14. We understand that talking is thinking aloud together.

15. We are going to try to beat each other in our group.

16. We will make group decisions that we can all agree to.

Worksheet 5 continued

Lesson 6 Science: similarities and differences

In the Talk Box	• An apple, a pair of scissors, a plant, a t-shirt, a percussion instrument, a toy, a torch (or similar range of items) • Worksheet 6: Creatures. One per group, cut into individual pictures

Learning objectives

To ask questions and make joint decisions based on reasons.
To observe features and categorise objects, recording and reporting findings.
To evaluate the effectiveness of the Talk Box Rules.

We are learning to look and think about things and notice what is the same and what is different.

Success criteria

I can explain what I notice about things. I can use what I notice to find ways to sort things into groups.

Whole class work 1

This lesson is about looking at ways things can be compared, using what can be observed and what we already know. Point out that we do not just use our eyes to find out about things but also our senses of touch, hearing and smell, and our memory. Revise the meaning of the words 'similar' and 'different' with the class.

Ask a child to choose two items unseen from the Talk Box.

Say what they look and feel like, and think of ways they are *similar* and ways they are *different* – generally, but also drawing on understanding of science concepts relating to living things, types of materials, and sources of sound and light as appropriate. Ask the child to turn their idea for saying how the things are similar or different into a question to ask a friend:

'Can you eat it?' 'What does it feel like?' 'Is it heavy or light?' 'Is it alive?'

Repeat this with a further two items.

Then pull out three items and put them into two groups on the basis of similarity or difference.

Reveal all the items and ask for suggestions as to how to put them into groups. Start by dividing them into two groups, then divide each of the grouped items.

Ask children to phrase their suggestions as a question.

Stress that there is no way to get this grouping exercise right or wrong, but that it is important to listen to people's opinions and see if you agree with them.

Ask the children to suggest similarities between things they have grouped as different.

Show and explain the learning objectives for this lesson.

Share the success criteria with the children.

Group work
Tell the groups that they are going to work together using the picture cards of creatures from Worksheet 6. Their task is to put the creatures into groups by looking at how they are the same or different.

Revise the Talk Box Rules and remind children to use the ground rules in their discussion.

They should be reminded particularly to ask one another questions about the creatures and to try to reach a group agreement.

Children in their groups first group the cards, shuffle them, then try to group them using different questions.

Whole class work 2
Ask a spokesperson for each group to explain how they have grouped the creatures. Are there any similarities in the class answers?

What were the favourite questions or the questions groups thought worked best? Choose an example of a group of creatures and ask for suggestions of another creature not in the pictures provided which might belong to the group, and one that definitely would not.

Ask what sort of groups of animals the children already know – such as pets, farm animals, zoo animals.

Ask the children to think about how these groupings can be open to question, such as, can a cat be a zoo animal (remind them about lions)?

Are donkeys farm animals?

Are snakes and tarantulas really pets?

Are the group of creatures we call insects always a nuisance?

Revise and model uses of 'similar' and 'different'.

Ask the children why they think people put things in groups.

Use the success criteria to discuss whether the learning objectives have been met.

Important: Ask the class to decide if the Talk Box Rules helped the groups to work together well. Should the rules be changed?

Extension activity 1: Classifying science objects

Resources

Talk Boxes, one per group, containing sets of material (at least ten items) relevant to the science context you have been teaching:

Science 2: Four different sorts of leaves; a lemon, orange, apple; something made of wood; stone; pictures of an insect, a mammal, a person; a flower; yellow plastic, orange plastic

Science 3: Two objects made from each of metal, plastic, wood, stone/rock; squares of two fabrics, paper, card; a cork; cling wrap; fur; cuddly toy; packet of sugar/salt; a picture of some people; a book; rubber; a pencil; a mug; a computer disk

Science 4: Candle, torch, small bulb, wire, battery; pictures of the sun, moon, a streetlamp, fire; penny whistle/recorder, percussion instruments, stringed instrument if possible, a small open box with elastic bands stretched around it; squeaky toy; shiny paper, shiny spoon

---

Learning objectives and success criteria

As before.

Group work

Remind the children to use their Talk Box Rules.

Ask the children to sort the objects (start by sorting into two groups, then sort the things within the groups) by using a *question with a Yes or No answer*:

For example, is it hard? Is it rough? Suggest that they recall what they have learnt in science and think of questions to do with that.

Ask the groups to decide on what they think is the best way of grouping the objects and why.

Ask groups to report their ideas to the class.

Create displays with the materials organised into a key or branching database with the Yes/No questions to read.

Extension activity 2: Virtual pond dip

Learning objectives and success criteria

As before.

Ask the groups to use their ground rules for talk to work with web-based resources. Observe features and group pond animals.

http://www.naturegrid.org.uk/
http://www.microscopy-uk.org.uk/ponddip/index.html
http://www.wildkids.org.uk/pondlife/ponddip.htm
http://web.ukonline.co.uk/conker/pond-dip/pondbugs.htm

Extension activity 3: Follow up for individual reasoning (and assessment)

Resources

Provide each child with Worksheet 6, scissors, paper and glue

Ask the children to look for similarities and differences among the creatures on the sheet.

Without discussing their ideas, ask the children to sort the creatures into two groups.

Decide what Yes/No question they would ask to categorise the creatures this way (e.g. 'Has it got four legs?' 'Has it got wings?').

Record their question in their own way.

Now look at one of their two groups of creatures.

Think of similarities and differences.

Sort the creatures into two groups again.

What Yes/No question would they ask to categorise the creatures this way? Record their second question (e.g. 'Is it furry?').

If required, ask the children to glue the creatures to show how they are grouped.

Reporting to a group, a partner or an adult

Ask the child to explain how they grouped the creatures and give reasons for their decisions. Encourage the child to ask their Yes/No questions and check with them that the categorisation works.

Extension activity 4: Using science language

Design Talk Box lessons using science vocabulary.

Encourage groups to use appropriate language and reasoning, working on questions such as:

- What can we observe?
- What is our investigation question/What are we trying to find out?
- What is our prediction?
- How can we find out?
- What do we notice from our findings?
- How can we share our ideas with others?
- What would we do differently next time?

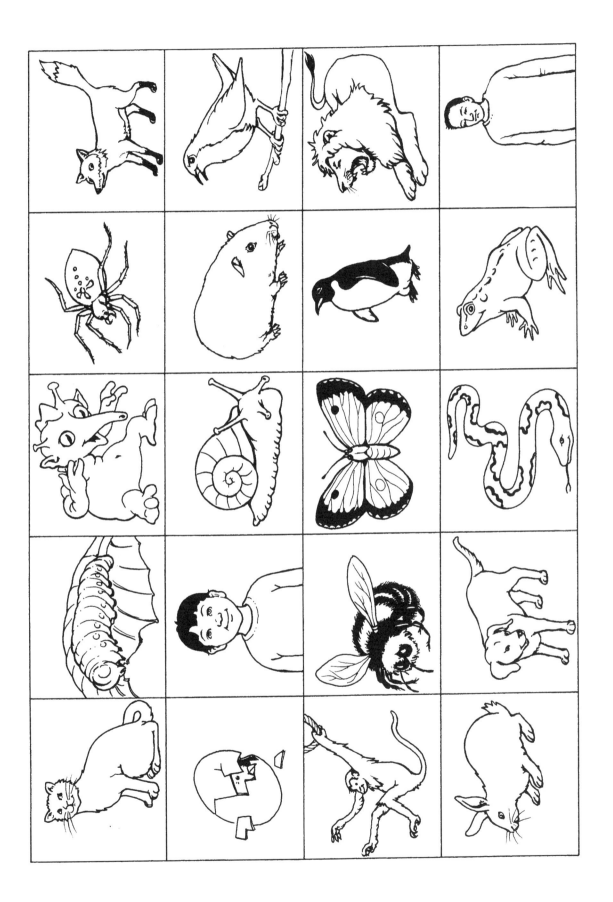

Lesson 7   Citizenship: choosing presents

Teacher's note

This is a citizenship lesson. It encourages children to see things from another person's point of view by providing discussion activities based around the idea of giving presents. This is a 'safe' context in which to learn the skills of thinking about other people and realising that their perspective is as valid as your own – and should be considered with interest, and respected. Further scenarios for discussion are suggested.

In the Talk Box

- Lots of toys: cars (different colours and models); box of blocks; cuddly toy/pony/teddy; Barbie; electronic toy; jigsaw; bat and ball; pictures of scooter/bike etc.
- Worksheet 7a Choosing presents – one for each group
- Worksheet 7b People cards (pictures of people – baby, eight-year-old girl and boy, twins, friends, granny, dog, mum) cut up – one set for each group

Learning objective

To become able to consider alternative points of view and reasons for them.

Success criteria

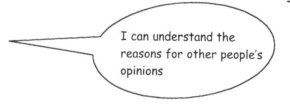

I can understand the reasons for other people's opinions

We are thinking about different points of view and using reasons to explain them.

Whole class work 1

Look at the toys in the Talk Box. Ask children to describe the toy, what it looks like, what it does; and say who they think it might belong to and why. Explore the children's reasons and ask for justification (e.g. for such ideas as cars are for boys; cuddly toys are for babies). Explain to the children that they are going to think about giving people presents. Ask them to suggest how other people choose presents to give them for a birthday, for example, drawing out the concepts of respecting the ideas, opinions, tastes and personalities of other people. The idea that some sorts of toys are 'better' (that is, usually more expensive) or 'silly' (that is, toys such as dolls) should be sensitively addressed.

Ask the children to recall the Talk Box Rules. Explain that they will be working in a group and should try to use the rules to think about each other's ideas, and to use the information to make their best decision.

Show and explain the learning objectives for this lesson.

Share the success criteria with the children.

The task for the group is to talk together to choose a present that a particular person will enjoy, and to consider the reasons for their decision. Shuffle the People cards (Worksheet 7b) and ask a member of each group to choose one without looking.

Group work

Ask the children to think about the toys in the Talk Box. Talk together to decide what the group would give to this person as a present. Give reasons and consider each other's ideas before making a decision. If all the toys are unsuitable, or a toy would not be an appropriate present, what else would the group suggest?

Next ask the group to imagine having the choice from a whole shop. If they could choose anything at all, what would be the choice for this person? Why?

The group complete Worksheet 7a Choosing presents then collect a new people card to talk about.

Whole class work 2

Ask groups to compare decisions for each of the people cards, and consider alternative points of view. The groups can state their choices and reasons for choices, and say whether they found it possible to come to a group decision. Stress that there are no right answers. Ensure that the discussion respects different opinions amongst the class, and respects the interests of the 'recipients' on the people cards.

Use the success criteria to discuss whether the learning objectives have been met.

Decide if the Talk Box Rules helped the groups to work together well. Should the rules be changed?

Extension activity 1: Name cards

Resources

Worksheet 7b People cards
Name cards (page 46)

Ask the children to recall presents they have been given and who gave them.

Tell the children that they have been asked to help choose a present. They cannot choose exactly what they would like because they have been given some money by someone else, and have to decide what present *they* would like to give. The group 'has' £5 to choose a present on someone else's behalf.

It does not have to be a toy. For example, a grandma, uncle or aunt might give a different present than a friend would.

Who is the present for? Ask a member of each group to take a People card.

Who is buying the present? Cut up the name cards, put them in the Talk Box and ask the group to draw one out.

Ask the group to use the Talk Box Rules to talk together and decide what they think the buyer would give, and why.

Name cards

Grandparent	The group
The Queen	The head teacher
A baby brother or sister	A friend
The person's pet	A neighbour

Extension activity 2: Follow up for individual reasoning

Repeat Extension activity 1 individually. Ask the child to draw a present for the person and to record a reason for their choice. Explain their choice to the group, partner or an adult.

Extension activity 3: Points of view

Ask talk groups to use the Talk Box format practised in this lesson to discuss issues of importance to your class. They can consider the point of view of others in such contexts as:

Choosing teams in games and PE

Who gets to choose? How does it feel to be chosen? To be left out? What are the problems for the leader? Or for the members of a team?

Taking turns, queuing and sharing equipment

How can things be organised so that it is fair for everyone?

Helping others to learn

If you help someone with their maths and they do better than you, do you feel annoyed or proud?

Joining in with others on the playground

How can we include everyone? How can people ask to join in? What are good ways to play together?

Possessions

Is owning a lot of things really important to make people happy? If someone has a better bike than you, or a more expensive game or toy, are they a better person?

Worksheet 7a Choosing presents

Who is the present for? (choose from People cards)	What present will your group choose? Why?	What other present would you choose? Why?

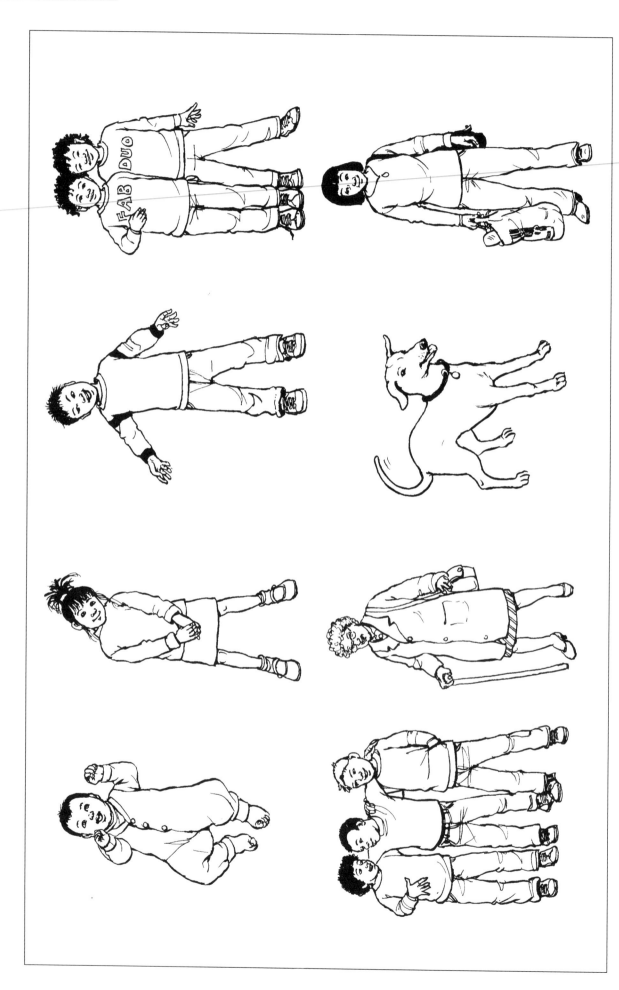

Worksheet 7b People cards

Lesson 8 **Pet shop**

In the Talk Box	• Models or pictures of pets – as many as possible. • Worksheet 8a What do the pets need? • Worksheet 8b Pet shop people

Learning objectives

To give reasons, evaluate evidence and compare ideas.
To recognise relevant facts.

> We are using things we think are important to give reasons and to make choices.

Success criteria

> I can say which things are most important and why. I can share my ideas and try to reach agreement.

Whole class work 1

Explain that the group are the owners of a pet shop. They have to make sure that people choose and take home a pet that will really suit them. If not, the animal may not be well treated. Invite children to choose a 'pet' from the Talk Box. Discuss with the class what each pet needs to be happy and healthy.

Ask the children to recall the Talk Box Rules.

Explain that they will be working in a group and should try to use the rules to think about each other's ideas, and to use the information to make their best decision.

Show and explain the learning objectives for this lesson.

Share the success criteria with the children.

Group work

The first discussion task is for the group to talk together to fill in Worksheet 8a, using ticks and crosses to indicate what they think each pet needs. Ask them to ensure that they agree on decisions.

The second task is to look at the people visiting the pet shop. Ask the groups to talk together to make decisions about which visitor should take which pet home. It is important to give reasons and for the group to think together to decide on the best reason.

Whole class work 2

Ask the groups to report and justify their choices.

Ask the children to comment on their group's use of the Talk Box Rules.

Was it easy or hard to use the rules? Were there any disagreements, and how were these sorted out? Should the rules be changed? Can anyone think of an example of a good reason given by a group mate? Who was a good listener? Who provided useful information (etc.)?

Which information about the people does *not* help you to decide?

(Picture cards include irrelevant information, for example whether there is a car, a mobile phone, a computer, etc.)

Use the success criteria to discuss whether the learning objectives have been met.

Decide if the Talk Box Rules helped the groups to work together well. Should the rules be changed?

Extension activity: Follow up for individual reasoning

Ask the children to work individually to think about a particular pet they would really like to have ('I must have this pet because . . . !') Draw the pet. Record what it needs. Record reasons why they should be allowed to own this pet – as persuasively as possible.

Try to persuade a partner, group or adult that they should have this pet. Ask children to identify which were the most persuasive reasons.

	Guinea pig	Dog	Parrot	Kittens	Fish	Gerbil
Garden						
Lots of space						
A walk						
Food every day						
Cleaning out						
Vet						
Company						

Worksheet 8a Pet shop: What do the pets need?

Anna

I am a gemini!

I'm going to be a vet!

football is cool!

I like chocolate – and shopping.

I ♥ my PS2

SPORT

Anton

I have a paper-round!

I don't eat meat!

my music!

my games!

I like skate-boarding!

my comics!

Tara

I am a teacher!

I like pizza!

I am Tara's rabbit!

I don't like birds!

pink gloves

I like to go for a walk

Gracie

I am 78!

I have 4 grandchildren

I watch TV a lot

I can't walk far!

I don't have a garden!

Kevin

I go to work

I like parrots

I drive fast!

I have a dog and a blue car!

size 10 shoes

Kevin

Tom + Laura + baby

We like to go to the park!

We don't have a car!

I like bananas!

We have a big garden

I am 5

blue pram

Worksheet 8b Pet shop people

Lesson 9   ICT and literacy: How to Catch a Pig

Teacher's note

The following lesson is written for use with specific software: *Kingscourt Inside Stories* (Set One). Please see page 55 for further in formation. It is included here either for use with *Inside Stories* if it is available in your school, or as an example of how Talk Box lessons can be used with ICT to support literacy. In this lesson the children are engaged in a meaningful task using software that provides real opportunities for talk. Other software in which members of a group compete with each other, where they must respond against the clock or where they have a straightforward choice of right or wrong answers do not usually provide contexts for Exploratory Talk. Children need to be reminded to use the Talk Box Rules and to try to reach agreement about their response as they move through the program.

In the Talk Box

- Pieces from a large jigsaw
- *Inside Stories* CD-ROM for Set One, Module 4

Also needed:

- Access to computers with printing facility for each group
- OHP or large board

Before the lesson, the children should have had an opportunity to use the CD-ROM to hear and discuss the story of the Three Little Pigs.

Learning objectives

To practise using the Talk Box Rules to reach decisions about solving a problem.

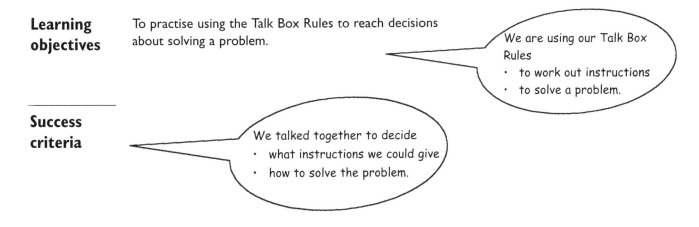

We are using our Talk Box Rules
- to work out instructions
- to solve a problem.

Success criteria

We talked together to decide
- what instructions we could give
- how to solve the problem.

Notes on loading

1. When you have opened the program choose *Played before*.
2. Select *Print a page* from main menu.
3. Select *How to Catch a Pig*.

Whole class work I

Take a piece of the jigsaw from the Talk Box. Show it to the children and ask for instructions about how to solve the puzzle of what its picture shows.

Show and explain the learning objectives for this lesson.

Share the success criteria with the children.

Revise the Talk Box Rules, discussing what each rule means. Tell the class that they are going to practise using these ground rules when they are working together in groups at the computer to solve a problem. Demonstrate the How to Catch a Pig activity to the class.

How to Catch a Pig

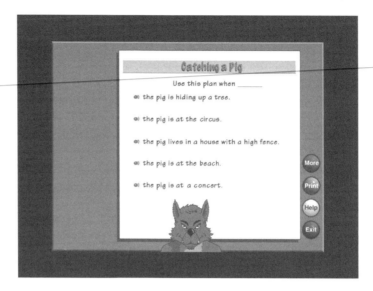

Explain that when the wolf appears, this is the signal for them to talk together about what to do before going on. Emphasise the importance of giving reasons and of making sure that everyone in the group has a turn to speak and to ask questions, before they reach agreement on their decision.

Practise doing this by working through the activity as a class. The children have to agree:

1. Where the pig is hiding
2. Which three things they will use to catch the pig
3. A set of instructions to explain their plan

When they have agreed on where the pig is and what they will use, they can print out a sheet similar to this one:

Computer printout

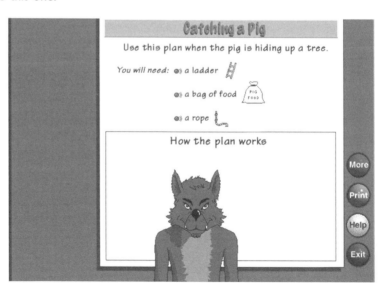

They then use this to record their instructions.

Discuss with the class how to record the instructions for their method of catching a pig. Work together through an example, emphasising the importance of using the Talk Box Rules to decide on each choice and each instruction.

Group work

Ask the groups to carry out the activity at the computer. Remind them about the importance of trying to reach an agreement before clicking on their choices.

Share the success criteria with the children.

As each group prints out the sheet, remind them to talk about their plan and agree each instruction, before one person in the group writes it down.

Whole class work 2

Ask each group to report back on their plans for catching a pig. Ask them to explain their choice of items to help them.

Use the success criteria to decide whether the learning objectives have been achieved.

Decide if the Talk Box Rules helped the groups to work together well. Should the rules be changed?

Extension activity: Follow up for individual reasoning

Ask children to work individually.

Record a set of instructions for a simple task, for example:

- Make a jam sandwich
- Tie shoelaces
- Lay the table
- Switch on the computer and find a file

Further information

Inside Stories is a product of Kingscourt/McGraw-Hill, Wimbledon Bridge House, 1 Hartfield Road, Wimbledon, London SW19 3RU, Telephone 020 8545 6690. Publisher: Mimosa Publications.

Lesson 10 Literacy: Climbing frame tag

In the Talk Box	• Playground pictures/model of climbing frame • Five pictures, models or dolls to represent the children • Toy dog • Green ball • One copy per group of: 'Climbing Frame Tag' story, Worksheets 10a, 10b and 10c

Learning objective

To use the Talk Box Rules to discuss issues, asking questions, sharing ideas and reaching a group agreement.

Literacy objectives: to consider different points of view; to devise story endings.

> We are using the Talk Box Rules to think together about different points of view about the same event.

Success criteria

> I can explain a point of view. I can talk with my group to reach agreement about choices.

Whole class work 1

Use Talk Box resources to talk with the children about trips to the park – if and why they enjoy going, and who with.

Explain the lesson aims and check that the children recall the Talk Box Rules.

Ask the children to listen carefully to the story 'Climbing Frame Tag'.

Before reading, show Worksheet 10c and provide this introduction to the story:

> There are five children in this story: Arsha, Erin, Declan, Vijay and Sally.
> While you are listening to the story, try to think of how the children might be *feeling* at different times. Are they happy, sad, upset, excited, friendly, cross?

Group work

Remind children to use the Talk Box Rules.

Ask the groups to discuss the story to complete Worksheet 10: 'Living graph'. This requires that they identify how people might be feeling as the story progresses, drawing smiley or sad faces to show feelings. They must ask for and provide reasons for opinions, and come to a group agreement.

Next ask each group to choose a story picture and choose a character.

The task is to talk together to decide what the character did, why it seems they did that and what they could have done instead.

Remind children to share all their ideas and to provide each other with reasons.

Whole class work 2	Ask groups to share their living graphs. Invite the groups to explain what they decided about the choices the characters made.
	What did the children in the story do and what they could have chosen to do instead?
	What would *you* do if you were, e.g., Declan or Erin? Can you say why?
	Ask groups to report how well they felt they worked together. Who asked a question? Did anyone have to change their mind about what they first thought? Can they think of examples of how they used the ground rules?
	Use the success criteria to discuss whether the learning objectives have been met.
	Decide if the Talk Box Rules helped the groups to work together well. Should the rules be changed?

Extension activity 1: Story telling	**Resources** Large paper and felt-tip pens

Learning objectives and success criteria

As before, but also to consider alternative points of view.

Group work	Ask the group to talk together to draw a picture:
	1. An ending to the story – what happens when Erin gets home? Where does the ball end up? What is the end of the story from Shep's point of view?
	2. Another episode of the story – what happens if Vijay is given a new ball to take to the park?
	Ask groups to make up a one-minute play or freeze frame which will show their story ending.

Extension activity 2: Follow up for individual reasoning	Ask the children to work individually.
	Choose a character from the story.
	Choose an episode from the story. Record how the character is feeling. Think what could happen to make their feelings change. What could another character do? Why? Record their new version of the story.

Extension activity 3: Follow up for individual reasoning	Ask the children to work individually.
	Think what they liked and disliked about the story and record this, with their reasons. For example, they could colour characters they liked green and those they disliked red, then record a reason. Explain their thoughts to a partner, group or adult. What are good reasons? What reasons do people share?

Climbing Frame Tag

Arsha, Declan and Erin were at the park. They were playing with Erin's green ball. They made up a really good game around the climbing frame, throwing the ball to each other and rolling it down the slide. Vijay came along and watched for a minute.

'Come and join in,' said Erin. She threw him the ball.

Vijay caught the ball, but instead of throwing it back to someone, he held on to it. Then he began to laugh and he ran away with the ball. The children called to him to come back, but he carried on running till he reached the far end of the park. Suddenly Erin, Declan and Arsha's game was over and they felt as if playing in the park was no fun any more.

Vijay played on his own with the ball for a while. It didn't seem a very interesting thing to do. There was no one to kick it to or to throw it back to him. Sally arrived in the park and watched him for a minute.

'Come and join in,' said Vijay.

Back at the climbing frame, the others were deciding what to do.

'He might have taken the ball but we can still play together,' said Arsha. 'We can start again and make up a new game.'

They all wanted to carry on enjoying running around with each other.

They began to play a sort of tag around the climbing frame, making up new rules and laughing when they got caught.

'Ok, I'll play,' said Sally to Vijay. Straight away he threw her the green ball. Sally caught it and ran away with it as fast as she could.

'Hey!' shouted Vijay. He ran after Sally but she was very fast. He had to stop and watch her go: he knew he'd never catch her. Now he was on his own again, with no one to play with and nothing to do. Kicking a stone, he made his way slowly back to where the others were having fun around the climbing frame.

'Hey! Where's my ball?' called Erin.

'Sally took it off me,' said Vijay.

'Oh, just come and play,' said Declan. 'We can get it back later.'

'I don't know the rules,' said Vijay.

'You learn them by playing. We just change them if we like,' said Arsha. 'All you have to do is go up the slide, not down, and I'm it, so you'd better run . . .' Vijay made a dash for the slide and in a moment they were all running and climbing and sliding. It was a good game.

Then they saw Sally running towards them, flying along as if she was being chased. The game stopped again. It looked as if she was coming to join in, but she took no notice of anyone, just ran right under the slide and hid herself there, making puffing noises to get her breath back.

'Ok, Sally! Where's the ball?' said Vijay. Sally didn't answer.

'What are you doing under there?' said Erin. Slowly, Sally slid out from her hiding place looking anxiously the way she had come.

'There was a dog, a horrible fierce dog,' she said. 'I was rolling the ball along and a big brown dog came and grabbed it and took it away! It barked at me and I thought it was going to bite – it didn't have an owner, there was no one I could ask for help.'

Declan climbed to the top of the climbing frame and looked around. He shook his head. There was no sign of a dog.

'It's gone now, Sally,' said Erin. 'You'd better stay with us for a while. It won't bother us if we're all together.'

Sally calmed down a bit.

'Sorry about your ball,' she said to Vijay. He looked a bit ashamed.

'It wasn't mine,' he said. 'I don't know whose it was.' The others looked at Erin, expecting she would be angry or upset with Vijay and Sally, but funnily enough she didn't seem too worried.

'I brought it to play with,' she said. 'But it wasn't mine. It belonged to our dog Shep.' Then she began to laugh again. 'You know what? I bet the brown dog was one of Shep's friends and Shep sent him to collect the ball back for him!'

They played the game of climbing frame tag together till it was time to go home.

Worksheet 10a How do the children feel?

	Arsha	Erin	Declan	Vijay	Sally
1. Climbing frame					
2. Vijay runs away					
3. Sally					
4. Tag game					
5. Sally runs away					
6. Vijay joins in					
7. Sally and the dog					
8. Erin and the ball					

Worksheet 10b Story scenes

Worksheet 10c Story characters

Sally

Vijay

Declan

Arsha

Erin

Lesson 11 — Maths: talking about patterns

In the Talk Box	• Examples of patterns and patterned material, such as wrapping paper, wallpaper samples, printed fabric, strings of beads, plain shapes, multi-link or other construction material in a variety of colours and/or shapes • Worksheet 11a: 'Pattern-making grid' – one for each group (or use squared paper) • Selection of counters or small bricks: each group will need 10–20 • Coloured pencils or felt tips

Learning objectives

Ask and answer questions to make choices and explain rules. Recognise simple patterns and relationships and make predictions about them, using correct mathematical language: turn, repeating, symmetrical.

We are learning to talk about patterns.

Success criteria

My group can agree on a set of rules to make a pattern. I can ask questions to find out about a pattern.

This lesson is about making and describing patterns. Revise with the class what is meant by the word 'pattern', and some of the mathematical terms for describing patterns: turn, repeating, symmetrical.

Now ask a child to take a sample of paper/fabric/beads out of the Talk Box. Ask the child to describe the pattern they can see. Now ask the child to think of a question they could ask about the pattern to a friend. Some examples of things to ask might be:

Does the pattern repeat – how?

Is the pattern symmetrical – how?

How might the pattern continue above, below or to the side of the sample?

Do any of the shapes in the pattern turn? If so, how much?

Repeat this process two or three more times.

Now take the bricks or construction material out of the Talk Box. Ask for volunteers to construct patterns using these objects. Can anyone guess the rule they have followed to make the pattern? Why do they think it is this? What would come next? Can anyone think of a way to change the rule? How?

Show and explain the learning objectives for this lesson.

Success criteria	Give each group a blank grid and a selection of counters or bricks (these should be a variety of colours and there should be more than ten per group). Now ask each group to decide on a pattern they could make with the counters. What rules will they make up to build the pattern? For example, 'You must have two of each colour together' or 'You can't have two of each colour together' or 'You must leave a space between each colour'. Explain that they will be choosing a pattern to show to the class and that people will ask each group questions to try to find out the rule they have chosen.

Share the success criteria with the children.

Give the groups a chance to find and make at least two patterns, then ask them to use the coloured pencils to record one of the patterns to show to another group.

Each group should now work with another group. Ask one group to show their pattern to their partner group. People in the partner group need to make comments and ask questions about the pattern, for example:

I think it is a symmetrical pattern because . . .

I think the next piece in the pattern might be . . . because . . .

Why was the third part of the pattern . . . ?

The first group should respond to the comments and questions, then the groups should swap roles.

Whole class work 2	Ask a child from each group to explain their pattern. Are there other groups that have used similar rules to create their patterns? For instance, more than one group may have used a rule involving symmetry or the use of spaces within the pattern. Were there rules that worked particularly well? Were some easier to follow than others? Were there any patterns that needed more than one rule to work? How were these patterns different from those that followed a single rule?

Use the bricks from the Talk Box again. Can anyone arrange them to make another pattern following their rule? Can anyone add another part to the rule? How would this change the pattern?

Look again at the success criteria.

Use these to discuss whether the learning objectives have been met.

Ask the class to decide if the Talk Box Rules helped the groups to work together well. Should the rules be changed?

Extension activity 1: Pattern making	Copy Worksheet 11b: 'Shapes for patterns' onto card. Cut out the shapes. (Use plastic shapes if available.) You will need enough shapes for the children to have one each.

Ask the children to work individually to think about a repeating pattern they could make with this shape. Ask them to draw round the shape to make a pattern. They may need to work through different draft ideas then choose their favourite to draw neatly.

Now ask the children to describe what is happening in their pattern to a partner, group or adult.

Ask the child to look at another child's pattern. Can they say what they think is happening in the pattern and give reasons for their ideas?

Extension activity: More patterns

Use your graphics program. Ask groups to make up and print a pattern with an explanation of how it repeats. Alternatively provide parameters for a pattern (e.g. only three colours: must use triangles and squares) and collect a range of different patterns as each group devises their own idea.

Worksheet 11a Pattern-making grid

Worksheet 11b Shapes for patterns

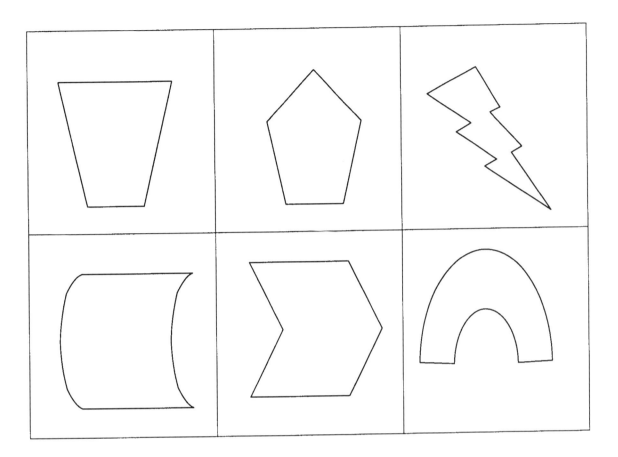

Lesson 12   Music: sound patterns

Teacher's note

This needs advance preparation.

Ask the children to bring in empty plastic soft drink bottles (330 ml) with screw tops.

Wash and allow to dry completely. In each put a small amount of dried rice, lentils, small stones and so forth, creating a range of shakers which are percussive (but not too noisy). Tape the tops on.

Secure a band of coloured paper round each shaker using three colours, e.g. red, green, blue.

In the Talk Box
- A range of percussion instruments
- Squared paper
- Felt tips or crayons

Learning objectives

Collaborate through talk to produce an original sound pattern.
Create and describe simple patterns and share ideas about them.

We are learning to talk about sound patterns

Success criteria

I can work with my group to make up and play a sound pattern

Whole class work 1

Ask three children to choose percussion instruments from the Talk Box. Ask all three to play the instruments together – this allows the class to experience sound with no pattern. Then ask each child to shake (tap, etc.) their instrument twice, in turn, and keep the turn-taking going. Show how this can be recorded by drawing the instruments.

Talk about making a pattern with the sound by following a rule, e.g. play once each; play twice each; once first time around, twice second time around; etc. Explain that everyone will be given a shaker and that by talking together the group can make up a sound pattern to play for the class.

Show and explain the learning objectives for this lesson.

Group work

Ask the children to remind one another of the Talk Box Rules. Explain that these are important because the task involves deciding together. Hand out the shakers so that each group has three different colours. Allow time for the children to play with the shakers and become familiar with the sound they make. Now ask children to play the shakers, red, blue, green, in turn. Record this pattern by drawing boxes on the board and colouring them or labelling red, blue, green. Ask children to suggest a new pattern. Try it and record by drawing.

The task for the groups is to talk together to decide on a pattern of sound using the shakers. These can be played in turn, or for some of the pattern two or three together. Record their pattern by colouring on squared paper.

Ask the groups to practise their pattern so that it is ready to be played for the class.

Share the success criteria with the children.

Whole class work 2

Ask the groups to play their patterns.

How are these different from one another?

Are there ideas that other groups would like to try out?

Can the recorded patterns be played by other groups?

Can groups say whether their ideas for a pattern changed as they talked about it and tried it out in their groups? Did this improve it?

Can a group play their pattern for the class using real percussion instruments?

Look again at the success criteria.

Use these to discuss whether the learning objectives have been met.

Ask the class to decide if the Talk Box Rules helped the groups to work together well. Should the rules be changed?

Extension activity 1: Silent shakers

Provide each child with a block, multilink, eraser, empty bottle – anything that is not too big and will not make a sound when shaken.

Ask the groups to talk together to make up a new pattern using the 'silent' shaker to introduce spaces into the music. Record by drawing a cross. So, for example, a sound pattern might be written:

R	X	G	G	X	B	X	B	X

Extension activity 2: Follow up for individual reasoning

1. Ask the children to work alone. Use their shakers to work out the sound pattern of a song that they know. Practise playing this. Ask individual children to play their sound pattern to the class. Who can guess what the song is?

2. Ask the children to make up a pattern on their own and record it. Say why they liked the pattern they created.

Discuss with the class whether they found it easier to work as a group than to undertake the task alone.

Lesson 13 Speaking, listening, learning

Teacher's note

This lesson requires advance preparation.

This lesson provides a context for your own speaking, listening, group discussion and drama objectives. The short story 'Ribby Rabbit' is used to provide context for sessions in which children work in their talk groups to achieve learning objectives based on those in the QCA *Speaking, Listening, Learning* guidance.

Please access the Speaking, Listening, Learning web pages at: www.standards.dfes.gov.uk/primary

Decide which of the four areas you wish to concentrate on. Select an appropriate learning objective for your year group. Some of the objectives are complex and may require division into two or three separate objectives, for separate lessons. Consider the story, or a story or poem of your choice. Devise an appropriate activity (example follows).

The lesson begins with you reading the story and explaining to the children exactly what the chosen learning objective means and how they can work together to achieve it.

Example 1: Using Ribby Rabbit with QCA Speaking and Listening objectives

> **In the Talk Box**
> - Toy rabbits, pictures of rabbits
> - Worksheet 13a: Rabbit finger puppets

Learning objective

We are learning to speak and listen so that we can learn.

Success criteria

We can share our ideas through talk.

Whole class work 1

Ask children to select a rabbit from the box. Give it a label to make it one of the rabbits in the story. You will need nine children to hold these rabbits while the story is being read, or give one rabbit to each group. Alternatively all children can have rabbit finger puppets.

Ask children what they know about rabbits – story rabbits or real ones.

Show and explain the learning objectives for this lesson.

Share the success criteria with the children.

Group work	Read the story 'Ribby Rabbit' (page 72) and ask the children to hold up the character rabbit when it appears in the story.
	Ask the children what they thought of how Ribby and Kipling behaved.
	State your Speaking, Listening, Learning objective and explain what this means.
	Ask the groups to carry out the activity you have devised. For example:
	Talk together to make up the next scene.
	Act out the story as a play.
	Draw Ribby and use a dictionary and thesaurus to write ten describing words around your picture.
Whole class work 2	Ask the class to share their work. Concentrate on deciding whether and how the learning objectives have been achieved.
	Use the success criteria to discuss whether the learning objectives have been met.
	Decide if the Talk Box Rules helped the groups to work together well. Should the rules be changed?

Example 2: Using a poem to devise a Talk Box Speaking, Listening, Learning Activity

---

In the Talk Box
- One copy of Worksheets 13b: Poem and 13c: Talking Points per group
- Coloured pencils or felt tips
- A selection of 'little creatures' (see Worksheet 13a 'Poem': pictures or models of frog, goblin, alien, mouse, worm, pixie, hobbit etc.)
- Tape/CD with suitable music, e.g. theme from *Lord of the Rings*; Enya song; short piece of flute music

---

Learning objectives and success criteria	For you to decide.
Example 3: Group discussion	Year 1: to ask and answer questions, make relevant contributions, offer suggestions and take turns
	Year 2: to ensure everyone contributes, and reach agreement
	Year 3: to actively include and respond to all members of the group

Ribby Rabbit

Ribby always wanted to be first in the queue. All the rabbits in Miss Thistle's class were fed up with him. Whenever they had to stand in a line to go for lunch or to come in from the playground, Ribby would rush to the front, shoving everyone else out of the way.

'Me first! Me first!' shouted Ribby.

There were seven rabbits in Miss Thistle's class; Ribby and his twin sister Blackberry; and the triplets Kipling, Lemony and Muzzle. There was Bramble Bunny who was always getting into trouble, and Skipper who was very clever.

On Monday, Miss Thistle asked the class to line up for break.

'Me first!' shouted Ribby, hopping up so fast that he knocked over the basket of coloured pencils. They all scattered on the floor and their points broke. Everyone had to help pick them up. Ribby stood at the door, keeping his place, and looking very hot and bothered.

On Tuesday, Miss Thistle asked the class to line up to have their photos taken.

'Me first!' shouted Ribby, shoving his chair back so hard that it crashed to the ground. Skipper picked it up for him. Ribby was so determined to be first that he didn't have time to do it himself.

On Wednesday, Miss Thistle asked the class to line up for assembly.

'Me first!' shouted Ribby, leaping to the door in such a rush that he knocked Lemony over. She banged her paw and started to cry. Suddenly Kipling lost his temper. He jumped up and shoved Ribby very hard, and Ribby fell down. Bramble Bunny saw this and thought it wasn't fair, so he rushed up and pushed Kipling over. Then Muzzle dashed across and knocked Bramble down – and suddenly all seven rabbits were tumbling around the classroom.

It took Miss Thistle and the class quite a while to sort it all out.

'Right. That does it,' said Miss Thistle. 'We are going to have to sort you out, Ribby.'

On Thursday, Miss Thistle said, 'Ribby, please stay in your place. Everyone else line up for lunch.'

The rabbits got themselves into a nice line. Ribby felt very cross. He frowned so hard that his ears stood straight up.

'Now Ribby, please join the end of the line,' said Miss Thistle.

Ribby was even crosser. He stamped his feet (and don't forget that a rabbit's feet are rather large).

'It's not fair!' he said to Kipling, who was just in front of him.

'Hey, don't worry so much,' said Kipling. 'What does it matter?'

Ribby couldn't explain why it mattered. But it did. They all went outside for lunch. Fluff was giving everyone dandelion sandwich and chocolate cake. Ribby was last in line. When it was his turn, Fluff said, 'Are you the last? You might as well have all of this, then!' and she gave

Ribby a really big slice of cake. It was lovely. After lunch, Miss Thistle came outside.

'Please come here and sit down, Ribby,' she said. He sat on the grass until all the others had lined up.

'Please join the back of the line, Ribby.'

Ribby didn't like everyone going in before him. His ears began to go up again. But as he went through the door, the Head Rabbit Mr Marjoram came along. Ribby held the door open for him.

'Well, thank you Ribby,' said Mr Marjoram. 'Will you take a message for me? Tell Miss Thistle and the class that Swizzle the story-teller will be arriving in half an hour.'

This was great news. When Ribby told Miss Thistle and the others, they were all very excited and pleased with him. It was almost as if he had organised the treat himself.

The bell rang.

'Please line up for the story-teller!' said Miss Thistle.

Ribby jumped up.

'Me fir . . . !' he began. But something funny had happened. All the other rabbits had lined up - but they'd left a big space at the front of the line. They were keeping the place at the front specially for him. Ribby wasn't so sure he liked this.

'Why are they all trying to make me go first?' he thought. 'It must be because no one else wants to be first. Perhaps it isn't a good thing to go at the front!'

He ignored the space and went to the end of the line.

'Ribby, you are funny,' said Kipling. Ribby, who was the last to sit down on the grass, got a big space to himself. They all enjoyed Swizzle's story.

On Friday, Miss Thistle was looking forward to a quiet day with everyone having a nice time in class. It was sunny outside and the bees were humming about.

At half past ten she said, 'Please will everyone line up for break?'

Then it happened.

'ME LAST!' shouted Ribby, dashing to the back of the classroom and tipping over two tables on the way. 'ME LAST!'

Worksheet 13a Rabbit finger puppets

Worksheet 13b Poem

Read the poem together.

Fairy Story

I went into the wood one day
And there I walked and lost my way

When it was so dark I could not see
A little creature came to me

He said if I would sing a song
The time would not be very long

But first I must let him hold my hand tight
Or else the wood would give me a fright

I sang a song, he let me go,
But now I am home again there is nobody I know.

Stevie Smith

Rogers, M. (ed.) (1987) *A Children's Book of Verse*. Newmarket: Brimax Books. ISBN 0-86112-426-X

Worksheet 13c Talking points

Use your Talk Box Rules to think together and help your group decide.
Make sure everyone is asked for their ideas.
Make sure everyone is asked for their reasons.

Talking points

We know what the little creature looks like! We can draw it here and write some describing words.	We know what song to sing! We can write our ideas here.
We can think of scary things! We can draw four things that might be frightening in the wood at night.	We can think of magic! We can draw a magic _____to help us in the wood. We can say what it does.

We know what has happened! We can share ideas. This is our idea about what happened to make everyone at home seem like a stranger:

We know what happens next! This is our idea:

We can share stories about when we were scared. On the back of this sheet we can draw a picture of each of us in our group:

(Each draw your picture and a smiley face when you've told a story about being scared.)

Lesson 14 Geography: children around the world

Teacher's note

This lesson can act as a template for a range of geography, history and citizenship contexts.

In the Talk Box	• A selection of everyday classroom objects, e.g. colour pencils, a writing book, book, maths game, whiteboard pen, child's storage tray, CD-ROM, calculator, small PE equipment, and items of clothing, e.g. school sweatshirt. • A collection of photographs of children at school around the world. One source for this is *Wake up, World! A Day in the Life of Children Around the World* by Beatrice Hollyer, published by Frances Lincoln in association with Oxfam (ISBN 0-7112-1480-0). Some of the images from this book relating to school can be seen at: http://www.oxfam.org.uk/coolplanet/kidsweb/wakeup/school.htm • Three contrasting photographs for each group – these should be of everyday events in the lives of children around the world such as images of children at mealtimes and at play. • Worksheet 14 (optional).

Learning objectives

To identify similarities and differences.

To describe accurately.

To give and listen to explanations.

> We are learning to look for similarities and differences and to explain them accurateky to each other.

Success criteria

> I can say how things are the same and how they are different. I can explain my ideas to the group.

Whole class work 1

Ask a child to take an object out of the Talk Box and say what it is. Ask children to talk together to consider how important it is in their school day. Could they manage without it? What else could they use if they did not have it? Repeat this activity two or three more times with the other objects.

Ask them to look around them at what is in the classroom. What have they used that day? What equipment do they like using? Why?

Share the learning objectives with the children.

Now show two photographs of children in other countries in a school setting. Explain that they are photographs taken of children similar in age to the class. Ask the children to talk together to share their ideas about things that they think are similar between the photographs, and which are similar to their own experience of school. When groups have had a chance to share their ideas with the whole class, repeat the activity. This time ask the children to look for and articulate any differences they can see between the photographs and their own experience.

Now show a third picture. Ask the children to compare all three photographs, pointing out similarities and differences. Encourage a positive approach to events and people in the pictures, stressing the similarities between the children in the pictures and themselves.

Ask the children to recall their Talk Box Rules.

Share the success criteria.

Group work

Provide each group with three photographs of children going about their daily lives. Ask the children to talk together to:

1. Describe to one another what they can see happening in each picture.
2. Look for similarities between what is happening in each picture and their own lives. Also, identify differences.
3. Use their understanding of the pictures to create a title for each.

Worksheet 14 can be used to support this discussion; but remind children that no written answers are required.

Whole class work 2

Ask each group to show one of their photographs and share their description of it, and their title, with the class.

Ask children to describe interesting similarities and differences, and to say what they see in the photographs that they would like to do or take part in themselves.

Use the success criteria to discuss whether the learning objectives have been met.

Did the Talk Box Rules help? Should they be altered?

Extension activities

1. Display photographs and the children's titles. Take photographs of your class playing and working. Ask the class to agree titles for these and add them to the display.

2. Ask groups to compile a brief bullet-pointed list to describe things that are similar in all the photographs. Alternatively, provide Post-It notes and ask groups to note similarities and differences to stick on the display.

Extension activities for individual reasoning

Ask children to bring in photographs. Share these out and ask children to describe activities in a given photograph or to compare two photographs.

Ask children to compile a list of describing words for a photograph, then display both photograph and words.

Ask children to write a paragraph, story or poem about the photograph, or to draw and describe an extension to the picture – what do they think is happening outside the frame?

Ask children to describe what might have happened just before this photograph was taken or what might happen next.

Children who have lived in other countries can be asked for their experiences of living somewhere different.

Worksheet 14 Talking points for pictures and photographs

Talk together about each of these talking points. Remember to ask for everyone's ideas, opinions and reasons.

Describing a picture

We can describe the people in the picture. They are . . .
We can describe the place. It is . . .
At the front of the picture is . . .
In the background is . . .
The colours and shapes are . . .
The sounds you might hear if you were there are . . .
The weather is . . .
The time of day or time of year is . . .
We like this picture because . . .

Similarities and differences

The places in the pictures are similar to here because . . .
The places in the pictures are different to here because . . .
The child in this picture is like us because . . .
All these children are similar because . . .

Making up a title

We think the title for this picture is . . . because . . .

End note from the Thinking Together Team

We hope that you and your class have found the Talk Box lessons useful and interesting.

For further information about other publications, or to find out about our training sessions for teachers, please contact:

Professor Neil Mercer
The Open University
Walton Hall
Milton Keynes
MK7 6AA

E-mail: n.m.mercer@open.ac.uk

There is also more information on our website: www.thinkingtogether.co.uk